The Secrets to Singapore's
World-class Math Curriculum

©2020
Wenxi Lee

Editor
Kristina Barile

Proofreader
Alexis Arceo

Consultant
Grace Anne Francis Wood

Design & Typesetting
Mark Chan (markcwy.com)

All rights reserved. Without limiting the rights under copyright reserved above, no part of this publication may be produced for economic purposes, stored, or introduced into a retrieval system, or transmitted in any form or by any means (electronic, mechanical, photocopying, recording, or otherwise), without prior written permission of the copyright holder.

*To my mama,
the best math teacher
I've ever had;*

*To my dad,
who taught me
that the pen
is always mightier
than the sword.*

Contents

1   **Preface**

3   **Introduction**

    3   Where in the world is Singapore?

    7   At the top of international education charts

CHAPTER 1

13   **What is Singapore's Math Curriculum (SG Math) All About?**

   14   A brief history of Singapore's mathematics curriculum

   17   Key components of Singapore's mathematics curriculum

CHAPTER 2

35   **Current Challenges Facing SG Math Implementation in the U.S.**

   36   **Problem 1:**   There is a lack of recognition that Singapore and the U.S. are two fundamentally different countries.

   41   **Problem 2:**   There is a lack of information about SG Math in the U.S.

CHAPTER 3

45   **Myths of SG Math**

   45   **Myth 1:**   SG math is not a spiral curriculum

   51   **Myth 2:**   I must buy manipulatives to use SG math

   54   **Myth 3:**   I have to follow exactly the structure of all instructional materials

   56   **Myth 4:**   The Model Method is the only way to solve problems in SG Math

   57   **Myth 5:**   SG math looks so simple that children can learn it on their own

CONTENTS

CHAPTER 4

61 The Real Takeaways of SG Math

62	**Takeaway 1:**	Invest in elementary mathematics education
70	**Takeaway 2:**	A logically and coherently structured mathematics curriculum is key
75	**Takeaway 3:**	Emphasize problem-solving processes
77	**Takeaway 4:**	Procedures are important, but they do not have to be memorized
80	**Takeaway 5:**	Practice, practice, practice!
82	**Takeaway 6:**	Integrate test-taking techniques in math lessons
84	**Takeaway 7:**	Develop children's mathematical mindsets
86	**Takeaway 8:**	Commit to a curriculum and stay flexible

CHAPTER 5

89 How do we implement SG Math more effectively in the U.S.?

90	**Action Item 1:**	Do more research
90	**Action Item 2:**	Invest in instructors
92	**Action Item 3:**	Drawing bar models is not an option; it's a necessity
92	**Action Item 4:**	Open up the problem-solving process
93	**Action Item 5:**	Focus on processes and teach error analysis
94	**Action Item 6:**	Engage children in your teaching
94	**Action Item 7:**	Encourage children to discuss math
95	**Action Item 8:**	Make connections between different topics
95	**Action Item 9:**	Expect children to do well in math
96	**Action Item 10:**	Let children apply concepts in different contexts

98 **Summary of Key Points**

99 **Notes**

105 **Bibliography**

Preface

When I graduated from college, I never thought I would end up pursuing mathematics education as a career. I worked for two years at an advertising agency as a data analyst and thought I had landed my dream job. My role was the perfect intersection of my two seemingly conflicting majors – mathematics and art history – in which I could crunch numbers and analyze images. Perhaps it was fate, but everything changed when I chanced upon the opportunity to tutor students using Singapore's math curriculum in the U.S.

I was initially puzzled when I heard about the U.S. implementation of Singapore's math program because it never occurred to me that my childhood math education had been unique. When my first student brought in the *Primary Mathematics* textbook and workbook, I felt both a wave of nostalgia and a sense of surprise that these materials have not changed for twenty years. My shock then turned to concern after I found out that my students were not taught some of the concepts and problem-solving strategies essential to Singapore's approach.

My curiosity led me to research how Singapore's math curriculum is being implemented in the U.S. Currently, the curriculum is copied and pasted into the American system with only slight modifications to align it to Common Core and state standards. The curriculum is also often explained to parents and educators in a cookie-cutter, theoretical way. I have observed in many implementations of Singapore's curriculum that the emphasis on getting all the "right" materials, such as textbooks, workbooks, teacher manuals, overshadows the need to understand the practical application of the curriculum in Singapore. This poses a major obstacle in adapting the program appropriately to an American context because education does not exist as a solely theoretical field. Education is deeply empirical and personal. It requires practical experience and, oftentimes, full immersion to truly understand what a curriculum really is.

It is through a praxis lens that I conceptualized this book. I wanted to break the mold of how Singapore's math curriculum is currently being discussed in the U.S. by integrating the personal and practical aspects of the curriculum within its theoretical framework. I truly believe that Singapore's program, when properly understood and applied, can greatly benefit American children and supplement math education research in the U.S. I hope you will join me in my journey as I share my perspectives and reflections on Singapore's math curriculum as a student and as an educator. Together, we can harness the power of an innovative and effective curriculum to transform children's lives.

Introduction

Where in the world is Singapore?

Singapore is a small country in Southeast Asia, about a 20-hour plane ride away from the U.S. For slightly over a century, Singapore was the crown colony of the British empire. After a short merger stint in 1963 with its neighbor, Malaysia, Singapore became an independent nation on August 9, 1965. Even though Singapore's name is derived from the Malay word Singapura, which means "lion city," the country is now a manmade paradise. Everything is so new and modern in Singapore that it is set as a futuristic vision of Los Angeles in the third season of HBO's *Westworld*.

Like the U.S., Singapore is a melting pot of cultures and ethnicities. While its population is often categorized into four major races - Chinese, making up about 76% of the residents, Malay at about 15%, Indian at 7.5% and people of Eurasian or other descent at 1.5%[1] - the multitude of ethnicities, religions, and even languages within the formal racial categories are also recognized. The diversity in Singapore's society is also what makes the city known for its fusion-style food, earning it the reputation of a food paradise.

However, unlike other countries in Asia, English is Singaporeans' *lingua franca*, a bridge to promote racial harmony. This makes Singapore a tourist-friendly and an incredibly international city because almost everyone you meet in Singapore can speak fluent English, and the official language of administration is English as well.

Unlike the U.S., Singapore is no larger than a "little red dot," as the locals affectionately call it, on the world map. At 280 square miles (or 725 square kilometers²), Singapore is about 3.5 times the size of Washington D.C, and slightly smaller than the five boroughs of New York City combined. Yet, despite this, Singapore is home to nearly 6 million people, about the size of the Chicago and Houston populations combined. This makes Singapore one of the densest territories in the world.

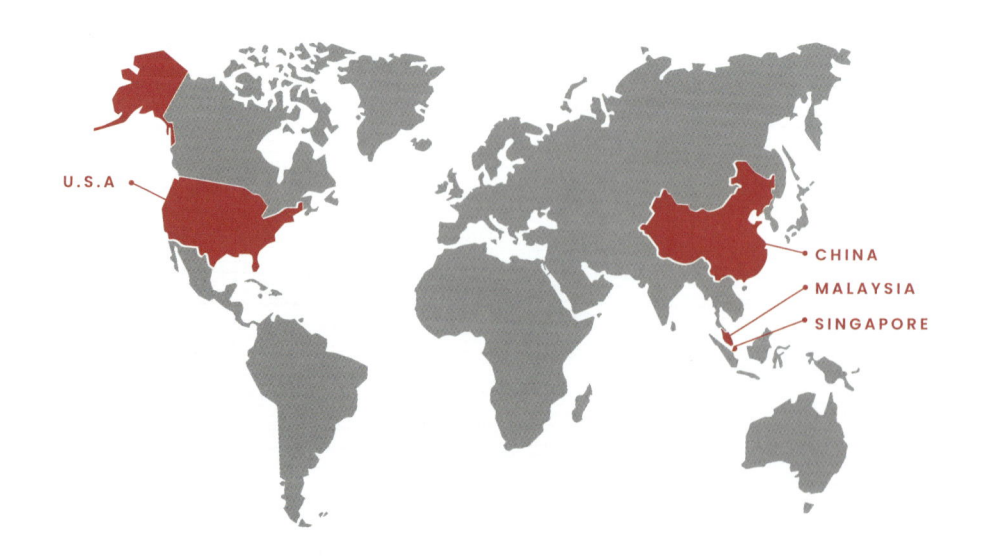

FIGURE 1 ▼
World Map

Despite its small size, Singapore is world-famous in many arenas. Its rapid and successful economic development since 1965 is deemed an extraordinary feat by global scholars, economists, and policymakers. When Singapore achieved independence, its GDP per capita was US$516.[3] Singapore quickly underwent industrialization and joined Hong Kong, Taiwan, and South Korea in the ranks of Four Asian Tigers. By the 1990s, Singapore's GDP per capita had risen to more than US$13,000[4], surpassing Germany in 1997.

Today, Singapore's nominal GDP per capita is more than US$65,000, the eighth highest in the world, just one rank lower than the U.S.[5] As a country that has only 0.007% of the land area and 1.7% of the population of the U.S., Singapore's comparable GDP per capita with the world's superpower is indeed nothing short of a miracle.

In addition to its high GDP per capita, Singapore was ranked first in the World Economic Forum's Global Competitiveness 2019 Report and oscillates between first and second place in the World Bank's index for ease of doing business. In December 2015, Singapore was reported to have the world's fastest internet. Changi International Airport, complete with its butterfly garden and indoor waterfall, has been the World's Best Airport for the eighth consecutive year, with Singapore Airlines ranked second best in the world. In fact, Singaporeans love to win so much that there is a local saying *kiasu* that literally means "scared to lose."

For all the state-of-the-art facilities and fast internet that Singaporeans enjoy, it comes as no surprise that there is a hefty price to pay. Singapore is consistently at the top of the world's most expensive cities in the world to live in. Imagine paying upwards of

SIN
SINGAPORE

LAND AREA
280 MI^2

GDP PER CAPITA
~$65,000

TOTAL POPULATION
5,600,000

CHINESE	MALAY
76%	**15%**

INDIAN	OTHERS
7.5%	**1.5%**

WORLD'S #2 AIRLINE

WORLD'S BEST AIRPORT

FOOD PARADISE

ONE OF THE MOST EXPEN$IVE CITIES IN THE WORLD

CHANGI AIRPORT

THE MERLION

MARINA BAY SANDS

GARDENS BY THE BAY

INTRODUCTION 7

US$70,000 for a Toyota Corolla Altis, which is an even more compact version of the Toyota Corolla!

Among all the accolades that Singapore has accumulated over the years, the most important and relevant one for this book is its rankings in international education assessments. Its unexpected, consistent success in the Trends in International Mathematics and Science Study (TIMSS) and Programme for International Student Assessment (PISA) catapulted Singapore's math curriculum to international fame.

At the top of international education charts

The TIMSS is a series of assessments organized by the International Association of Evaluation of Educational Achievement, conducted once every four years. It assesses 4th and 8th graders from various countries on their mathematics and science knowledge. Singapore wowed the world when it participated in the 1995 TIMSS, beating 29 countries and coming in first for both 4th and 8th grade mathematics. It has stayed at the top of TIMSS charts ever since.

TABLE 1 ▼

TIMSS 4th grade mathematics scores and rankings of Singapore and U.S. (Data source: TIMSS & PIRLS International Study Center)

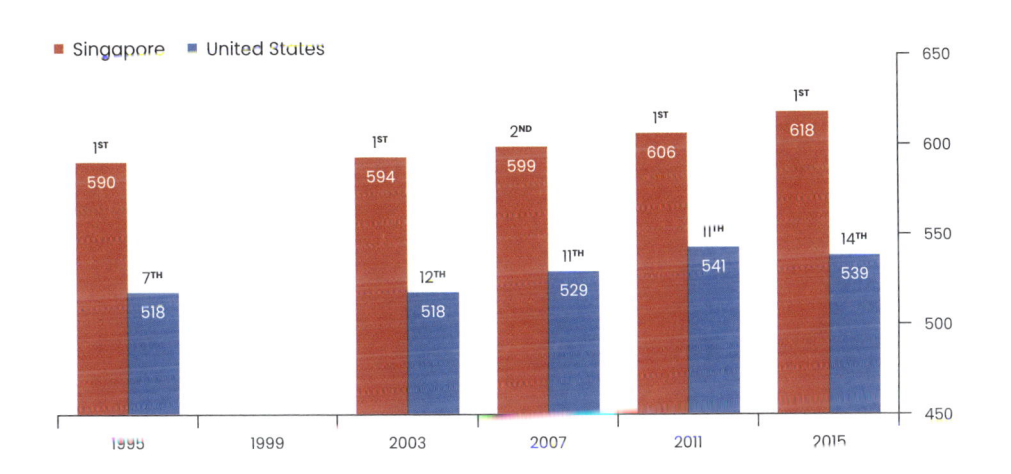

Year	Singapore	Rank	United States	Rank
1995	590	1ST	518	7TH
1999	—	—	—	—
2003	594	1ST	518	12TH
2007	599	2ND	529	11TH
2011	606	1ST	541	11TH
2015	618	1ST	539	14TH

THE SECRETS TO SINGAPORE'S WORLD-CLASS MATH CURRICULUM

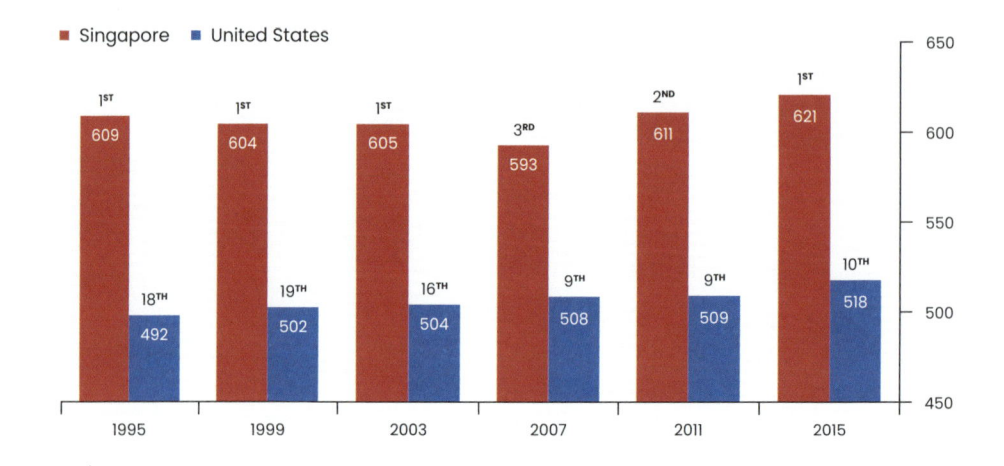

[Bar chart: TIMSS 8th grade math scores, Singapore vs United States]

Year	Singapore	Rank	United States	Rank
1995	609	1ST	492	18TH
1999	604	1ST	502	19TH
2003	605	1ST	504	16TH
2007	593	3RD	508	9TH
2011	611	2ND	509	9TH
2015	621	1ST	518	10TH

PISA, on the other hand, is a triennial assessment to test 15-year-old students in reading, mathematics, and science and is organized by the Organisation for Economic Co-operation and Development (OECD). Singapore is not a country in the OECD but has been highly ranked in all categories in every cycle of PISA since its first participation in 2009.

TABLE 2

TIMSS 8th grade math scores and rankings of Singapore and U.S. (Data source: TIMSS & PIRLS International Study Center)

TABLE 3

PISA reading scores and rankings of Singapore and U.S. (Data source: OECD)

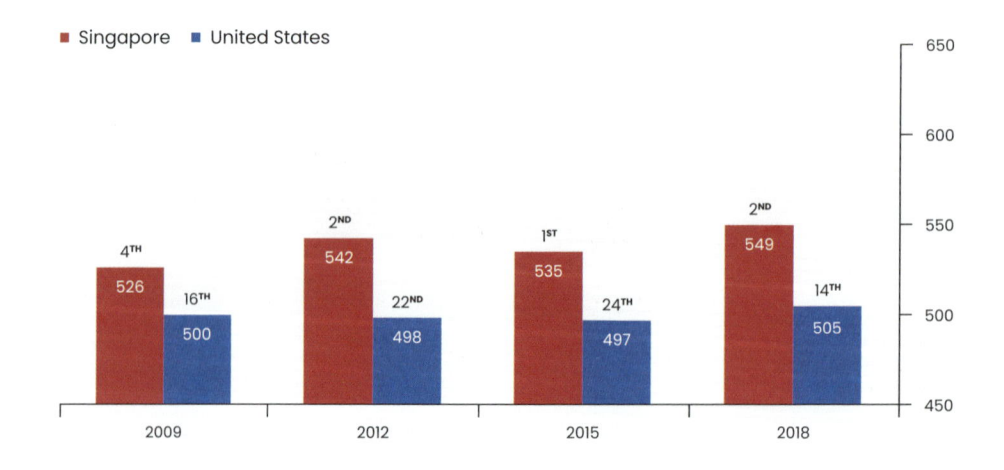

[Bar chart: PISA reading scores, Singapore vs United States]

Year	Singapore	Rank	United States	Rank
2009	526	4TH	500	16TH
2012	542	2ND	498	22ND
2015	535	1ST	497	24TH
2018	549	2ND	505	14TH

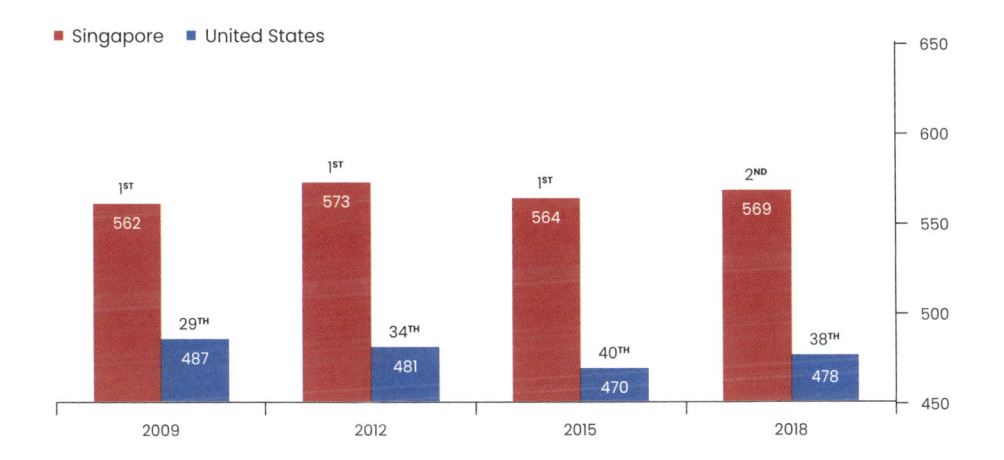

[Bar chart: PISA mathematics scores, Singapore vs United States]
- 2009: Singapore 562 (1ST), United States 487 (29TH)
- 2012: Singapore 573 (1ST), United States 481 (34TH)
- 2015: Singapore 564 (1ST), United States 470 (40TH)
- 2018: Singapore 569 (2ND), United States 478 (38TH)

TABLE 4
PISA mathematics scores and rankings of Singapore and U.S. (Data source: OECD)

TABLE 5
PISA science scores and rankings of Singapore and U.S. (Data source: OECD)

Singapore's prestigious ranking in mathematics, as you can see from Tables 1, 2 and 4, has attracted educators and policymakers from around the world, especially those from the West. In 2005, the American Institutes for Research (AIR) put together an ambitious comparative study for the U.S. Department of Education, which detailed insights from Singapore's math education system.[6] Extensive media coverage encouraged many parents and educators to adopt

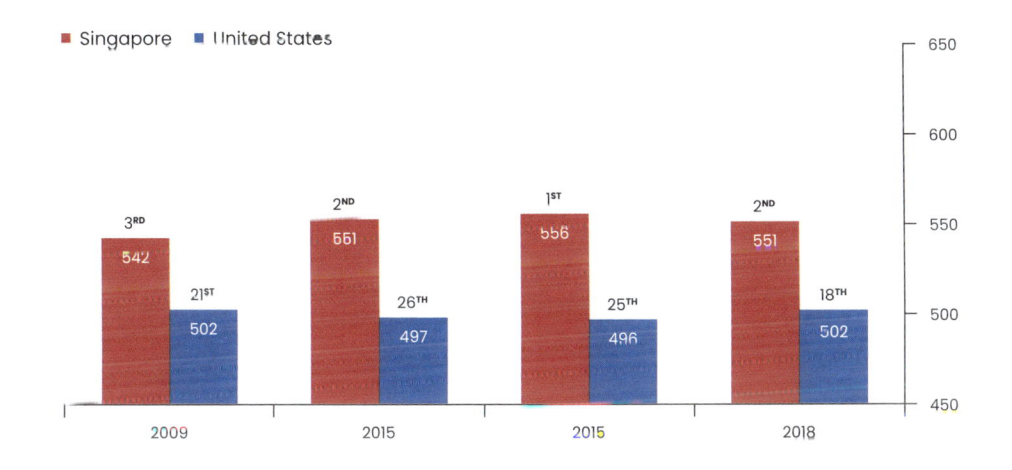

[Bar chart: PISA science scores, Singapore vs United States]
- 2009: Singapore 542 (3RD), United States 502 (21ST)
- 2015: Singapore 556 (2ND), United States 497 (26TH)
- 2015: Singapore 556 (1ST), United States 496 (25TH)
- 2018: Singapore 551 (2ND), United States 502 (18TH)

Singapore's math curriculum. However, after two decades, Singapore's approach to mathematics continues to be an enigma to many who are eager to emulate Singapore's success.

Because of Singapore's rankings, there is an expectation – a particularly unrealistic one in the U.S. – that American students will be able to achieve the same level as their Singaporean peers if they are also taught Singapore's math curriculum. Although this line of reasoning is tempting, it promotes the false belief that a good curriculum is the only component needed for children to excel in math.

A good math curriculum absolutely plays a crucial role in helping children succeed in math. However, apart from the curriculum, there are a variety of other reasons why Singaporean students rank so highly in math. And no, it has nothing to do with the stereotype that Asians are good at math. The 2005 AIR report points out one of the reasons: students in Singapore are exposed to much more challenging questions at an earlier age, as compared to their American counterparts.[7] Since TIMSS and PISA compare specific grade levels or age groups, it makes sense that Singapore ranks higher if its students are taught to solve more advanced math problems than American students at the same grade level. Another reason, highlighted by many critics of Singapore's math curriculum, is the ubiquitous presence of tutoring centers in Singapore. Many parents enroll their children in extra lessons after school, even if they are already performing well.

It is easy for many of us, myself included, to focus on the tangible elements, like test scores, when we are evaluating a curriculum. This is especially true in the case of math curriculums because this subject seems fairly neutral and objective. After all, 1+1=2 holds true no matter what language you speak or which country you come from. Therefore, it is particularly important to remember that a math curriculum exists within a complete education system. It does not exist in a vacuum.

Most education systems are fundamentally shaped by cultural and socio-political forces. This makes adopting a foreign curriculum very tricky. We need to understand the influences on the education system in which the curriculum was created, including the learning and testing materials. From what I have seen, after two decades of implementing Singapore's math program in the U.S, there is still a lack of consideration for the nuances of this curriculum. In order to adapt the program to the American context, we need to remind ourselves that Singapore and the U.S. are two distinctive countries with drastically different education systems, which means it is going to take a lot more than swapping out tropical images and the metric system to successfully adopt the curriculum.

When implemented successfully, Singapore's math program can be extremely useful to improve the level of math achievement in the U.S. However, the way in which it is executed has been ineffective because there is a superficial understanding of what it is and why it works. This book draws on my personal experiences as an individual who has gone through Singapore's education system, majored in math at an American university, and taught Singapore's curriculum in the U.S. Not only have I experienced firsthand the differences in math education between Singapore and the U.S., I have also observed American students being taught an inauthentic version of Singapore's math curriculum.

For many years, I have been motivated to write this book to demystify Singapore's approach to math for parents and educators who are already using, or interested in, the curriculum. More importantly, I want to demonstrate that Singapore's math program is so much more than just a curriculum; it embodies many important values, attitudes, and perspectives of what a good math education should look like. It is my hope that you will not only gain a deeper understanding of Singapore's math curriculum by the end of this book but that you will also be able to look at math education in a whole new light.

CHAPTER 1

What is Singapore's Math Curriculum All About?

Math is just math in Singapore, just like how American football is just football in America. The trademarked term "Singapore Math"[8] is coined in the U.S. and is used to differentiate the elementary math programs that use Singapore's approach from all the other math curricula in America. To make it easier to read, I will abbreviate Singapore's math curriculum as "**SG Math**" for the rest of this book.

The original program, designed in Singapore, is called *Primary Mathematics*, which is now published in three editions in the U.S. These are the U.S. edition, the Standards edition, and the Common Core edition. The U.S. edition is a direct adaptation of the version used in Singapore, covering grades 1 through 6. The Standards edition follows the U.S. edition closely, with some topics reorganized to align with the California state math standards. The Common Core edition, however, stops at grade 5 and is modified to cover topics required by the Common Core State Standards. Even though *Primary Mathematics* is the most authentic SG Math series in the U.S., it is actually no longer used in Singaporean schools. The two newer SG Math programs published in the U.S. are Houghton Mifflin Harcourt's *Math in Focus*, and Singapore Math Inc.'s *Dimensions Math*.

Let us look briefly at the history of Singapore's math curriculum before we dive deeper into the core components.

A brief history of Singapore's mathematics curriculum

Unlike the U.S., Singapore's education system is highly centralized and monitored at the top by the Ministry of Education (MOE), which is responsible for hiring teachers, teacher education, and curriculum development, among many other things. However, even though every area of the education system is now standardized, it hadn't always been this way.

Before Singapore's independence, schools were typically run by ethnic organizations that designed their own curriculums and specified their own language of instruction. As the nation gradually established its independent status, the government started to consolidate the control of schools and standardize the use of English in order to build a coherent educational policy. The first set of MOE-designated elementary math syllabi were made available for nationwide use in 1960, but mathematics was not made a mandatory subject through 10th grade until 1970.[9] Countless rounds of revisions were made to the mathematics curriculum until the 1980s, when many of the key components that are synonymous to the modern-day SG Math were developed.

The 80s was an important decade in Singapore's math education landscape. One of the key pedagogical approaches inspired by Jerome S. Bruner – guiding students through concrete-pictorial-abstract stages of mathematical learning – was added to the curriculum in 1981.[10] In 1983, Dr. Kho Tek Hong and his team created the landmark "Model Method" to help students solve word problems.[11] This method was initially intended only for students 4th grade and above but quickly gained traction to begin in 1st grade. Following these innovative pedagogical practices, MOE set up a syllabus review committee in 1988, which established the School Mathematics Curriculum Framework (SMCF) that continues to undergird the nation's curriculum to this day.[12]

Curriculum development in Singapore mostly stabilized by the mid-to-late 1990s, as evidenced by its TIMSS results starting in 1995, though minor tweaks were still being made regularly. Today, the curriculum retains many of the core components that were developed back in the 80s, and it continues to undergo revision every six years,[13] despite its high rankings internationally.

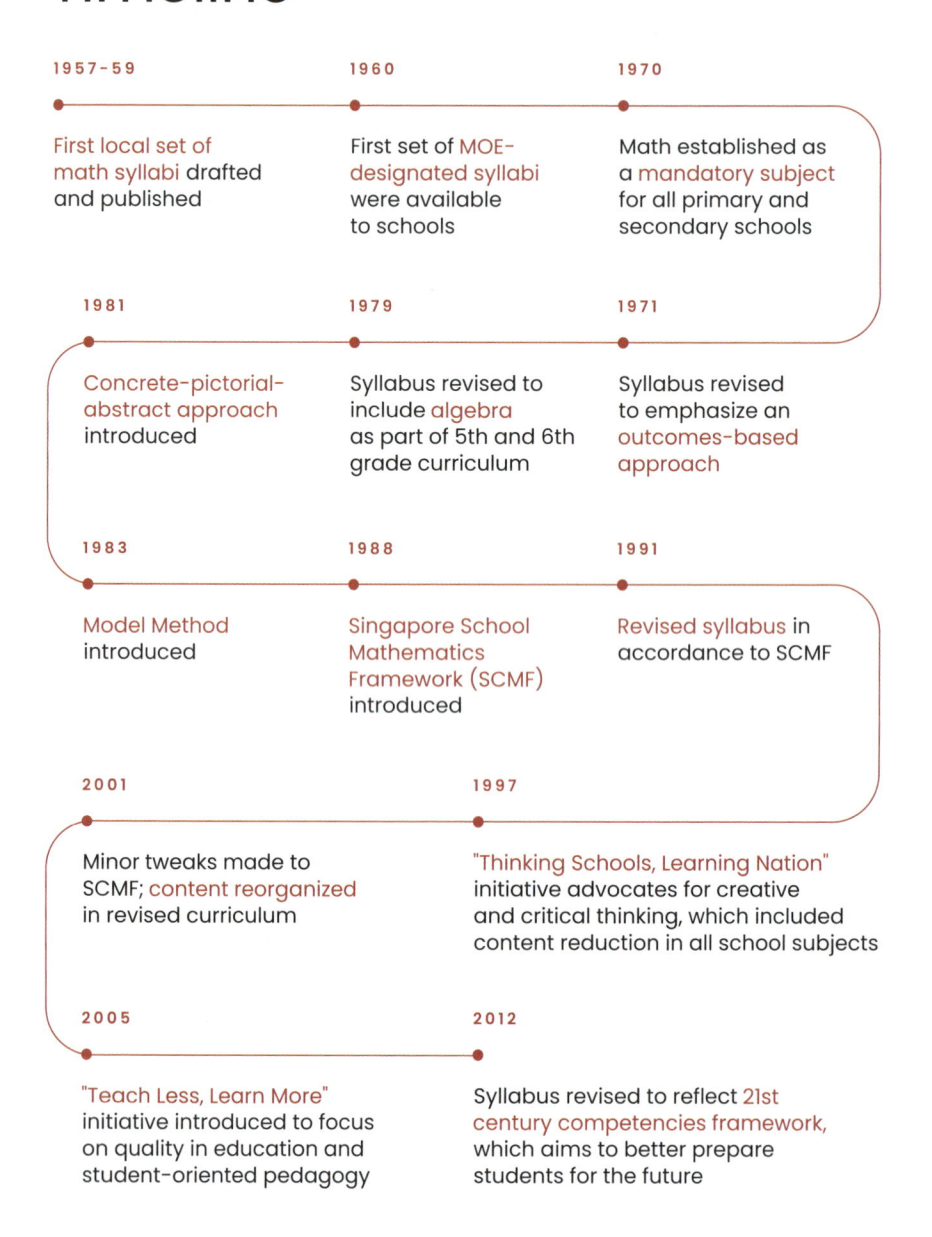

Timeline[14]

1957-59
First local set of math syllabi drafted and published

1960
First set of MOE-designated syllabi were available to schools

1970
Math established as a mandatory subject for all primary and secondary schools

1981
Concrete-pictorial-abstract approach introduced

1979
Syllabus revised to include algebra as part of 5th and 6th grade curriculum

1971
Syllabus revised to emphasize an outcomes-based approach

1983
Model Method introduced

1988
Singapore School Mathematics Framework (SCMF) introduced

1991
Revised syllabus in accordance to SCMF

2001
Minor tweaks made to SCMF; content reorganized in revised curriculum

1997
"Thinking Schools, Learning Nation" initiative advocates for creative and critical thinking, which included content reduction in all school subjects

2005
"Teach Less, Learn More" initiative introduced to focus on quality in education and student-oriented pedagogy

2012
Syllabus revised to reflect 21st century competencies framework, which aims to better prepare students for the future

Key components of Singapore's mathematics curriculum

The first impression that many people have towards Singapore's curriculum is that it is a fundamentally East Asian theoretical and pedagogical approach to teaching and learning mathematics, but that is actually not true at all. Singapore's curriculum is uniquely Singaporean in the sense that it is an amalgamation of ideas and theories borrowed from elsewhere. Nobody does it better than Singapore when it comes to adapting foreign concepts to local contexts. In the words of the founding Deputy Prime Minister of Singapore, Dr. Goh Keng Swee, "no matter what problem Singapore encounters, somebody, somewhere, has solved it. Let us copy the solution and adapt it to Singapore."[15]

When you look closely at the individual theories and ideas on which Singapore's curriculum is based, you will find that many of them originated from western countries, mainly the U.S. However, just because Singaporean officials often look elsewhere for inspiration and are rarely tasked with reinventing the wheel, it does not mean that they simply copy a policy or idea directly. The genius of curriculum designers in Singapore lies in their ability to dissect theories of well-known educational psychologists and researchers, which they then integrate into a comprehensive curriculum unique to the local context.

According to a professor at Singapore's National Institute of Education (NIE), Lee Ngan Hoe, there are two key approaches and two key features that define Singapore's mathematics curriculum.[16] I bet you'll be surprised to learn that Singapore's approach is essentially American at heart.

KEY APPROACH 1
Spiral Curriculum Approach

The spiral curriculum is based on the 1960 idea of Jerome S. Bruner, a renowned American educational psychologist. Bruner believed that a spiral curriculum allows for the introduction of big ideas to children of any age because it can foster the readiness to learn and provides the space for topics to be "developed and redeveloped in later grades."[17]

A spiral curriculum is very much like assembling a multi-tier cake. When you bake, you portion out the cake and filling evenly so that you don't use all of the parts on the first layer. Then, you build the cake by alternating the cake and filling layers; making sure it doesn't topple over becomes more challenging with every added layer.

Similarly, when you spiral topics in a curriculum, you don't want to teach everything about a single concept all at once. Instead, you want to break the concept down into manageable lessons so that children can build on previously-taught layers and be exposed gradually to increasingly challenging ideas.

Let me give you an example. Addition is a concept introduced to children in kindergarten or first grade. However, we do not expect children to know how to add 359 and 451 when they are six years old. What a good spiral curriculum does is guide children through the stages of adding one-digit numbers, then two-digit numbers, and eventually three-digit or any multi-digit numbers, along with other concepts such as place values. This way, children are not overwhelmed by having to add astronomical numbers together when they first learn the concept of addition. Over time, they are able to use what they have already been taught to deepen their understanding of addition, as well as perform more challenging calculations.

FIGURE 2 ▶

Singapore's spiral curriculum approach

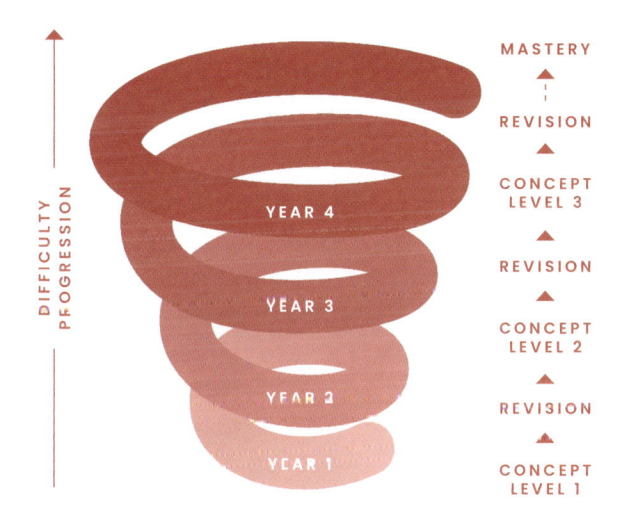

```
DIFFICULTY PROGRESSION →

YEAR 4
YEAR 3
YEAR 2
YEAR 1

MASTERY
↑
REVISION
▲
CONCEPT LEVEL 3
▲
REVISION
▲
CONCEPT LEVEL 2
▲
REVISION
▲
CONCEPT LEVEL 1
```

SG Math isn't the only math curriculum using a spiral model. In fact, a lot of math (and other subject) curriculums in the U.S. and around the world adopt this approach. What makes Singapore's spiral curriculum unique is that the topical framework for each grade level is age-appropriate and that all concepts introduced are interconnected, building a solid foundation for the next. This means that children are never expected to grasp concepts that are too advanced or too abstract for them. Instead, their knowledge is built systematically, layer by layer.

Unfortunately, because of how the topics are organized in the curriculum, Singapore's approach is often misconstrued as the opposite of a spiral curriculum in the U.S., especially when discussed in comparison to American math curricula such as *Everyday Mathematics* and *Saxon Math*.

This is one of the biggest myths of SG Math - a point I will discuss in detail in the next chapter.

KEY APPROACH 2
Concrete-Pictorial-Abstract (CPA) Pedagogical Approach

This crowd-pleasing approach that caters to visual and hands-on learners is yet another adaptation of Bruner's ideas. Interested in the "nature of intellectual development," Bruner theorized that we have to go through three systems of representation - action (enactive), visual or sensory (iconic), and language (symbolic) - until we are able to command all three.[18]

These three systems of representation serve as the theoretical foundation for SG Math's concrete-pictorial-abstract approach. In the concrete stage, children are given the opportunity to manipulate concrete objects and learn through action. When they move on to the pictorial stage, they transition from the objects they were handling to drawing out concepts. Finally, they advance to the abstract stage where they are able to use the mathematical language.

Like the spiral curriculum approach, the CPA stages are not only applicable to math. We have all gone through some kind of CPA learning journey in our lives, even if you did not use SG Math growing up. Language learning naturally occurs through the three stages. Babies love to point at the things they want. How many of us, as parents and adults, have brought an object to a baby when we finally figure out what it is they want and said the name of the object out loud as a teaching moment? As the babies grow to be toddlers, they can look at a picture of the object and recognize the corresponding word. The final stage of language development is when the child has added the word to their vocabulary and is able to use it freely.

CONCRETE

5 Cookies

PICTORIAL

Drawing of 5 Cookies

ABSTRACT

5

COOKIES

Math (5),
Language (Cookies)

FIGURE 3

Concrete-pictorial-abstract progression

SG Math is one of the few math curricula in the world that has applied CPA extraordinarily well by capitalizing on and prolonging the pictorial stage with bar model representations. Bar models are also known as the Model Method which, as we will see below, is a visual tool developed to help students solve word problems and strengthen conceptual understanding through pictorial representations.

KEY FEATURE 1
The Model Method

The Model Method is the crown jewel of Singapore's math curriculum. If you search for SG Math online, chances are the majority of articles will mention the Model Method as the distinguishing feature of the curriculum. If you recall, this method is a relatively recent innovation and has only been fully rolled out in Singapore schools since the early 90s. In fact, my peers and I were probably among the first few cohorts who were taught with the method since first grade.

The Model Method, also known as bar models or model drawing, refers to the use of rectangular drawings to visually represent and explore the relationships within a problem situation. However, it's not just a problem-solving tool; it also doubles as a visualization tool to strengthen conceptual understanding. According to Dr. Kho, the leading figure in the development of the Model Method, it has four features[19]:

1. To help students gain better insight into mathematical concepts such as fractions, ratios, and percentages

2. To help students plan the solution steps for solving an arithmetic problem

3. To employ a method that is comparable to, but less abstract than, the algebraic method

4. To stimulate students to solve challenging problems.

There are two basic models[20] in this method, which correspond to the types of common word problems presented in elementary school mathematics.

Part-whole models

The part-whole model is used to illustrate situations when the whole is made up of different parts. It is a fantastic way to teach number bonds in lower grades because it visually represents the concept that a number can be made of up two or more smaller numbers. Addition and subtraction are also concepts that bar models can teach effectively.

ADDITION PROBLEM EXAMPLE

Allison has 3 cookies. Her brother, Alan, has 4 cookies. How many cookies do they have altogether?

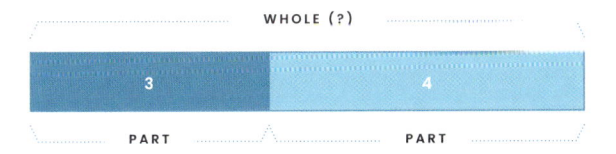

WHOLE (?)

| 3 | 4 |

PART   PART

Part + Part = Whole
3 + 4 = 7

SUBTRACTION PROBLEM EXAMPLE

Jacob has $10. He used $2 to buy a pen. How much money does he have left?

WHOLE ($10)

| $2 | $? |

PART   PART

Whole − Part = Part
$10 − $2 = $8

In upper elementary grades, the part-whole model can help children visualize multiplication and division word problems, as well as those that involve fractions, ratios, and percentages.

MULTIPLICATION PROBLEM EXAMPLE

Ben spent a quarter of his money on a toy car. If the toy car costs $10, how much money did Ben have originally?

WHOLE ($?)

$10

PART

One Part × Number of Parts = Whole
$10 × 4 = $40

DIVISION PROBLEM EXAMPLE

There are 100 chairs in 4 classrooms. A teacher wants to have an equal number of chairs in each classroom. How many chairs should be in one classroom?

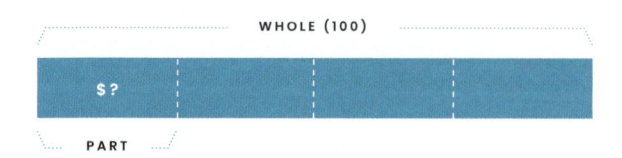

WHOLE (100)

$?

PART

Whole ÷ Number of Parts = One Part
100 ÷ 4 = 25

Comparison models

Comparison models demonstrate the relationship between two or more quantities when they are compared to show their differences. In lower grades, the comparison model is employed to teach relative quantities such as greater than, smaller than, biggest, and smallest, as well as word problems involving addition and subtraction.

ADDITION PROBLEM EXAMPLE

Ben has 5 books. Jacob has 10 more books than Ben. How many books does Jacob have?

[Bar model showing Ben: 5; Jacob: 5 + 10, with SMALLER QUANTITY, DIFFERENCE, and LARGER QUANTITY (?) labeled]

Smaller Quantity + Difference = Larger Quantity
5 + 10 = 15

SUBTRACTION PROBLEM EXAMPLE

Allison has 3 cookies. Her brother, Alan, has 20 cookies. How many more cookies does Alan have than Allison?

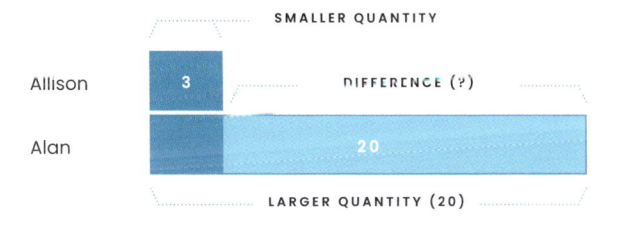

[Bar model showing Allison: 3; Alan: 20, with SMALLER QUANTITY, DIFFERENCE (?), and LARGER QUANTITY (20) labeled]

Larger Quantity − Smaller Quantity = Difference
20 − 3 = 17

As students advance to upper grades, comparison models can be used to solve word problems that involve multiplication and division, ratios, percentages, and fractions, as well as before-and-after scenarios.

MULTIPLICATION PROBLEM EXAMPLE

Jacob has 5 times as many books as Ben.
If Ben has 5 books, how many books does Jacob have?

SMALLER QUANTITY

Ben — 5

Jacob

LARGER QUANTITY (?)

Smaller Quantity × Multiple = Larger Quantity
5 × 5 = 25

DIVISION PROBLEM EXAMPLE

Allison has 40 jellybeans. She has 5 times as much jellybeans as pieces of chocolate. How many pieces of chocolate does Allison have?

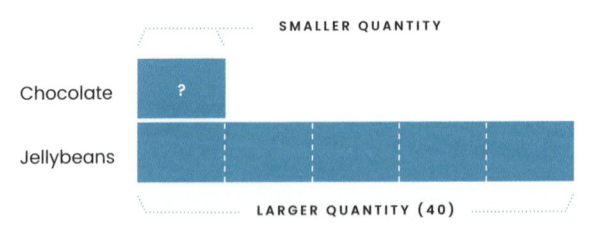

SMALLER QUANTITY

Chocolate — ?

Jellybeans

LARGER QUANTITY (40)

Larger Quantity ÷ Multiple = Smaller Quantity
40 ÷ 5 = 8

The above examples constitute only the basic forms of part-whole and comparison models. For more examples, I highly recommend you refer to *The Singapore Model Method for Learning Mathematics* published by Marshall Cavendish Education Singapore.[21] The beauty of bar modelling lies not only in its versatility in various mathematical settings but also in its ability to prolong the pictorial stage in the CPA approach through 5-6 years of elementary mathematics education. Teaching young children to use visualization techniques to solve math problems is crucial in helping them see the connection between abstract concepts and visual representations. More importantly, children will internalize the value of visualization in mathematical problem-solving and in other settings as well. In the age of big data, data visualization is a highly sought-after skill in every industry, but educators have yet to catch on that it is a skill that can be introduced and developed at a young age.

KEY FEATURE 2
The School Mathematics Curriculum Framework (SMCF)

This framework is much less discussed than the CPA approach or the Model Method in the discussion of SG Math in the U.S., but it is central to the curriculum. Not only does SMCF represent the philosophy of the curriculum[22], it also guides teachers on how to structure their lessons, as well as helps curriculum designers and policy makers design and revise the curriculum.

Figure 4 (1990 version)

Attitudes:
- Appreciation
- Interest
- Confidence

Metacognition:
- Monitoring of one's own thinking

Skills:
- Mental calculation
- Communication
- Arithmetic manipulation
- Algebraic manipulation
- Handling data
- Use of mathematical tools
- Estimation and approximation

Processes:
- Deductive reasoning
- Inductive reasoning
- Heauristics

Concepts:
- Numerical
- Geometrical
- Algebraic
- Statistical

Central: **MATHEMATICAL PROBLEM SOLVING**

FIGURE 4 ▲

1990 version of School Mathematics Curriculum Framework (Source: MOE[23])

Figure 5 (2012 version)

Attitudes:
- Appreciation
- Interest
- Confidence
- Beliefs
- Perseverance

Metacognition:
- Monitoring of one's own thinking
- Self-regulation of learning

Skills:
- Numerical calculation
- Algebraic manipulation
- Spatial visualisation
- Data analysis
- Measurement
- Use of mathematical tools
- Estimation

Processes:
- Reasoning, communication and connections
- Thinking skills and heuristics
- Applications and modelling

Concepts:
- Numerical
- Geometrical
- Algebraic
- Statistical
- Probabilistic
- Analytical

Central: **MATHEMATICAL PROBLEM SOLVING**

FIGURE 5 ▼

2012 version of School Mathematics Curriculum Framework (Source: MOE[24])

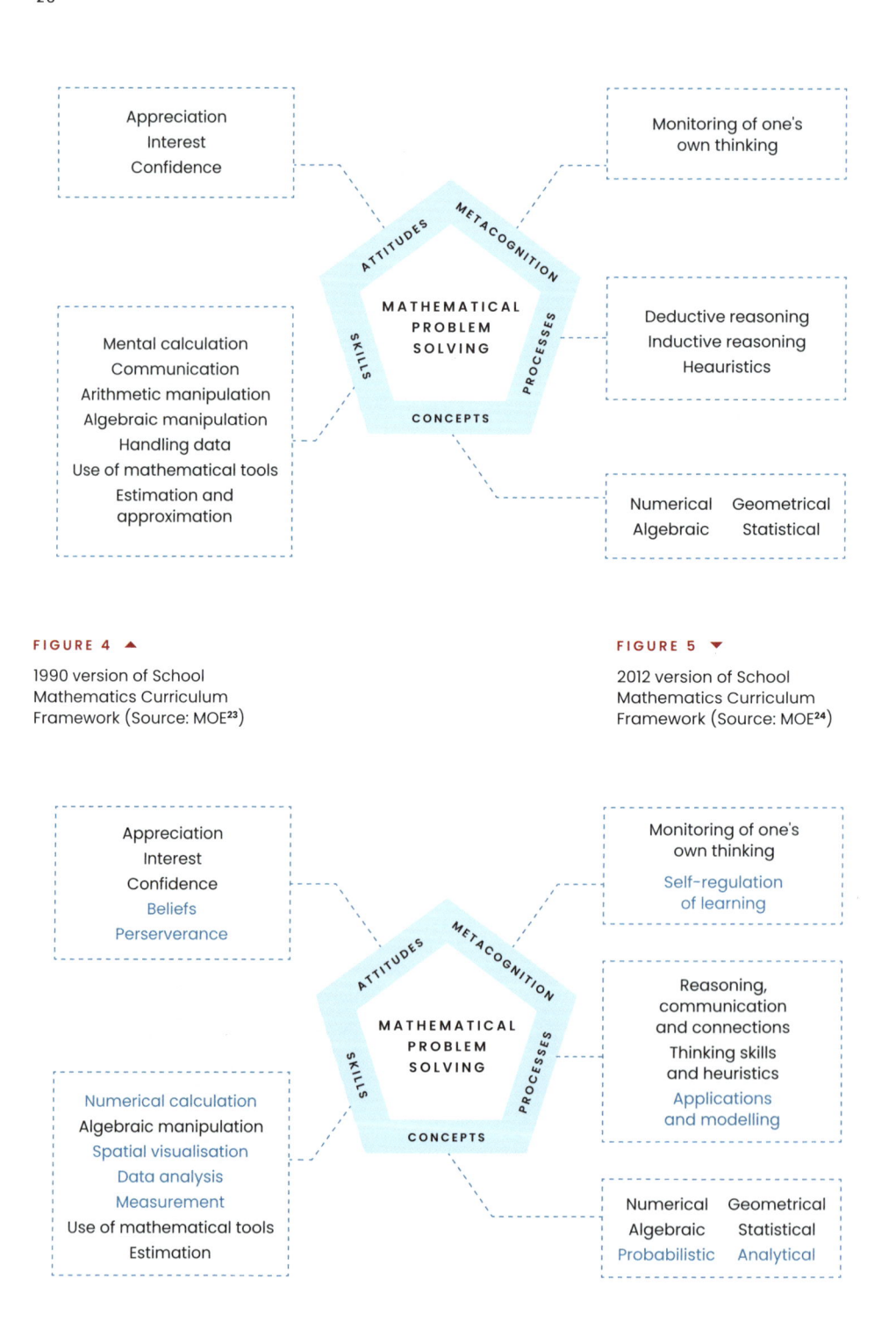

As shown in both figures 4 and 5, problem-solving is the focus of Singapore's curriculum, with five supporting components - concepts, skills, processes, metacognition, and attitudes, in both versions of SMCF. First published in 1990, this framework seemed to coincide with the five strands of mathematical proficiency formulated by the American National Research Council's Mathematics Learning Study Committee in 2001. Led by Jeremy Kilpatrick, the committee identified conceptual understanding, procedural fluency, strategic competence, adaptive reasoning, and productive disposition as the crucial components of a good math education.[25] Even though these five components are listed individually in the SMCF and the findings of the National Research Council, it is important that we recognize that they are interdependent and should be developed in tandem with each other.

Concepts (CONCEPTUAL UNDERSTANDING)

There is a strong emphasis on the mastery of concepts in Singapore's curriculum. It seeks to develop **inter-conceptual** connections, which encourage students to recognize the relationships *between* concepts, e.g. subtraction is the inverse of addition; it also develops **intra-conceptual** connectedness, which deepens children's knowledge *within* a concept,[26] e.g. the concept of addition isn't just about adding things together but is also about the understanding the various properties that hold true in all addition situations (See Figure 6). These two conceptual connections are very important because they make it easier for children to learn math in the long run. Oftentimes, children with strong conceptual understanding have "less to learn because they can see the deeper similarities between superficially unrelated situations."[27]

FIGURE 6 ▼

Inter- and intra-conceptual relationships between addition and subtraction

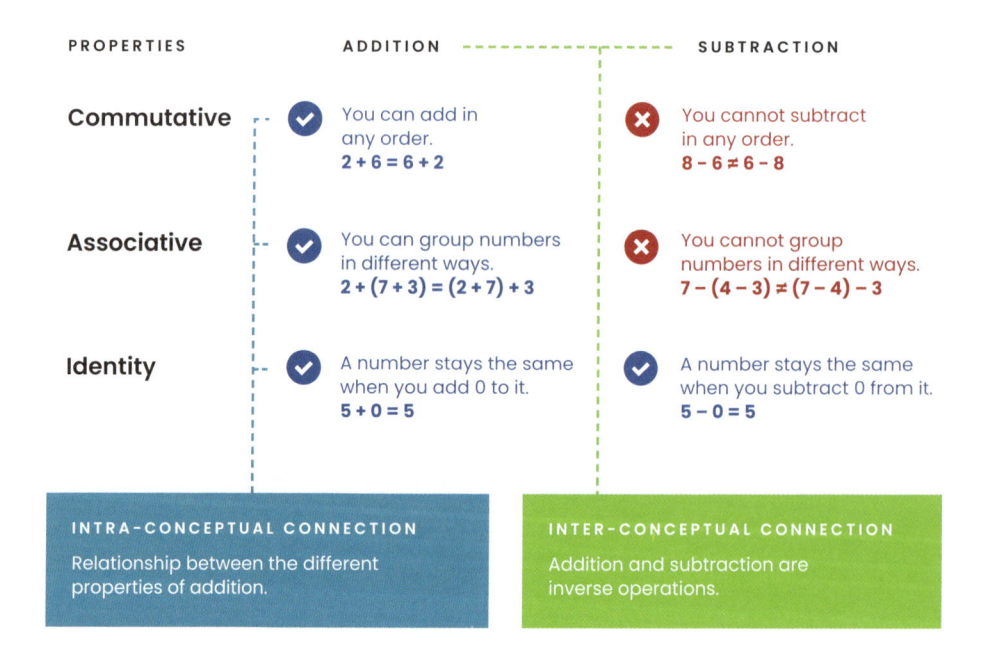

PROPERTIES	ADDITION	SUBTRACTION
Commutative	✓ You can add in any order. $2 + 6 = 6 + 2$	✗ You cannot subtract in any order. $8 - 6 \neq 6 - 8$
Associative	✓ You can group numbers in different ways. $2 + (7 + 3) = (2 + 7) + 3$	✗ You cannot group numbers in different ways. $7 - (4 - 3) \neq (7 - 4) - 3$
Identity	✓ A number stays the same when you add 0 to it. $5 + 0 = 5$	✓ A number stays the same when you subtract 0 from it. $5 - 0 = 5$

INTRA-CONCEPTUAL CONNECTION
Relationship between the different properties of addition.

INTER-CONCEPTUAL CONNECTION
Addition and subtraction are inverse operations.

Skills (PROCEDURAL FLUENCY)

Singapore's curriculum does not buy into the divide between the traditionalists and reformists of math education. Instead of debating whether mathematics instruction should focus on computation skills or higher-order thinking, Singapore's curriculum is designed to teach children both. Educators in Singapore recognize that the ability to calculate is as important as understanding the "why" behind the steps. Without a certain a level of technical skills, children are unable to work on higher-order reasoning skills and grasp more advanced concepts. Likewise, without conceptual understanding and the ability to reason mathematically, children are more likely to be weak in computation skills. Teachers in Singapore aim to promote conceptual procedural connections so that children have a relational understanding[28] of mathematics, which means that they understand how and why specific rules and procedures work.

Processes (STRATEGIC COMPETENCE)

The previous point about relational understanding goes hand in hand with developing children's strategic competence, which simply refers to the ability to solve problems. When children do not have a relational understanding of mathematics, they will find it challenging to tackle math problems, especially non-routine ones that they have never seen before. To nurture confident problem solvers, Singapore has adopted Hungarian mathematician George Pólya's four-step problem solving process[29] (See Figure 7).

There is also much emphasis on heuristics, which is a big word for problem-solving strategies, in Singaporean classrooms. Children are taught many different kinds of heuristics so that they are able to choose the ite strategy for each situation. The Mod- prime example of a heuristic, but take ot the only strategy taught in Singapore.

FIGURE 7 ▼

Pólya's problem-solving process

① UNDERSTAND THE PROBLEM
Read the problem, and note down key pieces of information.

② DEVISE A PLAN
What heuristic should I use? Should I draw bar models or should I use guess and check?

③ CARRY OUT THE PLAN
Solve the problem with procedures, formula or algorithms.

④ CHECK YOUR ANSWER
Check the solution.
Plug the solution into the question and see if everything makes sense.
Check computations.

Metacognition (ADAPTIVE REASONING)

Metacognition is a term coined by American developmental psychologist John Flavell in 1976. Influenced by the work of the famous Swiss educational psychologist Jean Piaget, Flavell built on Piaget's notion of intentionality in cognitive processes. Intentionality assumes that thinking is an active and deliberate process, which means that it is an act that can be monitored. Flavell conceptualized metacognition as the 'thinking about thinking,' involving an 'awareness of,' 'monitoring of,' and 'regulation of' one's thinking and learning.[30] The ability to monitor and regulate one's cognitive process is crucial in developing adaptive reasoning, which refers to the "capacity to think logically about the relationships among concepts and situations."[31] In order to justify why a certain strategy or procedure is used in a problem, children must be able to keep track of and analyze their thinking process to articulate their reasoning, both verbally and in writing, behind each step.

Attitudes (PRODUCTIVE DISPOSITION)

In the first version of the SMCF, attitudes only included an appreciation, interest, and confidence in math. In 2001, perseverance was added to the attitudes component of the framework. As documented in 1968 by Benjamin Bloom, an education professor at the University of Chicago, perseverance, also known as grit, is a crucial trait to develop in the process of mastering a skill.[32] This is because when we believe that we can improve a skill by spending more time and effort on it and never giving up, we are engaging in what Stanford psychology professor, Carol Dweck, deems a "growth mindset." Having a growth mindset is especially important in math because it helps us dispel the myth that many of us continue to believe in – that we are born with our mathematical abilities and that if we do not perform well in math, it means that we are simply not math people.

When Singapore added perseverance to the framework two decades ago, it seemed insignificant, but we now know how forward-looking that decision was. While we may be familiar with the notion of growth mindset now, Dweck's groundbreaking research was only published in her 2006 book – *Mindset: The New Psychology of Success* – five years after Singapore made the revision. In the realm of math education, the growth mindset concept really took off after Dweck's Stanford colleague, Jo Boaler, published *Mathematical Mindset: Unleashing Students' Potential Through Creative Math, Inspiring Messages and Innovative Teaching* in 2005. What this really means is that Singaporean children have had an enormous, 20-year head start compared to their American peers in establishing a growth mindset when learning math! And it really goes to show how essential mindsets and attitudes are when it comes to mathematical learning.

CHAPTER 2

Current Challenges Facing SG Math Implementation in the U.S.

According to one article[33], more than 2,500 schools in the U.S. and many more homeschool families have chosen to adopt SG Math in the past two decades. Numerous studies have been conducted to evaluate the effectiveness of textbooks[34] and pedagogical tools[35] based on Singapore's approach in American classrooms. The results of these studies are mostly positive, with noticeable gains made in student achievement and enjoyment of mathematics. However, because of various issues, such as budget and the lack of specialized knowledge in Singapore's approach, the curriculum has been phased out of many schools and districts even if there was substantial improvement. Homeschool communities that adopt SG Math usually face similar problems as schools and districts, although at a much smaller scale. Due to the lack of SG Math resources available to homeschoolers, many make the switch to another curriculum when they find it too difficult to use.

In this chapter, I will be identifying two major problems that I have observed in the current implementation of SG Math in the U.S. The first is the lack of recognition that SG Math is a curriculum designed for Singapore, which is a drastically different country than the U.S. Parents, educators, and publishers of SG Math materials in the U.S. have to take into account the differences in culture, attitudes towards education, and the broader education system to better adapt the curriculum to American children. The second problem is closely related to the first. Because the contextual gap between Singapore and the U.S. is not addressed, there is a lack of comprehensive and accurate information on SG Math that is available to the American public. This promotes misinterpretations of the curriculum, prevents people from grasping its true nature, and perpetuates many myths, which I will discuss in detail in the next chapter.

PROBLEM 1
There is a lack of recognition that Singapore and the U.S. are fundamentally different countries

As I have mentioned in Chapter 1, Singapore's education system is highly centralized and supervised by MOE. All instructional materials published for school-use must be approved by MOE, and the ministry organizes large-scale curriculum reviews regularly. Pre-service teachers are selected to attend the National Institute of Education (NIE), the only teacher training institution in Singapore. They are paid a salary by MOE during the entire course of their training and are required to serve a three-year bond at an assigned school. While the schools in Singapore have been given more autonomy in the past decade, it is important to note that all local schools are funded by the government and are considered public schools. The handful of private schools in Singapore that do not follow MOE's syllabi are international schools and are predominantly attended by foreigners.

Since the education system is under the central government's jurisdiction, Singapore has a unified vision of its education policies. Singapore continues to uphold the conviction of its first prime minister, Lee Kuan Yew, who famously proclaimed that "education is the key to the long-term future of any people."[36] Lee saw education as a way to build social unity and cohesion as well as a means for economic survival. This was especially relevant when Singapore was becoming an independent nation. For more than five decades, education has been consistently at the top of the government's fiscal spending priorities. Even in the aftermath of the financial crisis of 2008, the former finance minister of Singapore, Tharman Shanmugaratnam, announced that the education budget would not be cut, but instead increased from S$8.0 billion (~USD$5.84 billion) in 2008 to S$8.7 billion (~USD $6.35 billion) in 2009. He declared "education is a necessary investment in good times as well as in bad times,"[37] demonstrating that it is always important to invest in the future.

The philosophy that education is "an investment, not an expenditure"[38] runs deep in the nation's psyche. Not only does the government invest heavily in education, Singaporean parents are also determined to provide their child with the best possible education. While Singapore's education system is supposedly designed in a way that does not require additional remediation, local parents allocate a significant amount of money each month to enroll their child in the best tutoring centers in the country. This culture of extracurricular lessons can be largely attributed to Singapore's society as an "exam meritocracy."[39]

The message to children in Singapore is loud and clear: as long as you get good grades, you will have a bright future. It is no surprise then that many parents scramble to gather the best resources so that their children can have the opportunity to gain upward social mobility in Singapore.

On the other hand, the U.S. education system is decentralized. It is against the law for the U.S. Department of Education to specify a national curriculum[40], giving states and school districts complete autonomy over content taught in classrooms. There is a wide selection of textbooks and instructional materials available, many of which seek to satisfy every state's requirements. The various teacher training programs in universities across the nation are unable to prepare teachers for a standard teaching license valid in every state. Instead, teachers who move to another state may have to spend time and effort to obtain an additional state-specific license. Private schools, however, do not require teachers to obtain a teaching license and are funded differently than public schools. These variations in funding structures, teacher requirements, and curricula result in a system that has a wide range in quality and student achievements.

The emphasis on privatization in education reform in the U.S. further limits the government's role in education. Supporters of privatization claim that for-profit organizations are more capable of improving the quality of public schools by increasing competition and enabling parents to choose the best school for their child. In contrast, critics argue that turning over public education money to private organizations undermines the education system since privately managed schools are not subjected to the stringent scrutiny of federal and state agencies in the same way that traditional public schools are. Public school districts are often subjected to budget cuts, especially after President George W. Bush's No Child Left Behind (NCLB) Act, which allocates funding according to the student test scores in each school.

The issue of privatization in the American education system is only one of many that are widely debated, and there seems to be no consensus on what the solutions should be. The decentralized nature of the American system results in multiple, and often conflicting, visions of how children should be educated. This polarity in views is also apparent in the actions of parents and educators when they choose the kind of curriculum to implement.

FIGURE 8 ▼

Singapore vs. American Education System

SINGAPORE VS. AMERICAN EDUCATION SYSTEM

SINGAPORE

| Ministry of Education | 1. Teacher education
2. Curriculum design
3. Approval of instructional materials | → | Schools |

UNITED STATES

Federal US Department of Education
× 50 States
→ State Level Board of Education
1. Teacher education
2. Curriculum design
3. Creation of standards
→ City & District Level
→ Home Schools
→ Public & Charter Schools
→ Private Schools

The state of mathematics education in the U.S. parallels its education system. The only semblance of a national mathematics curriculum is the standards published by the National Council of Teachers of

Mathematics (NCTM) and the Common Core initiative, but states and school districts retain the power to structure their own curricula. Mathematics education is also polarized by the perspectives of the traditionalists and reformists, where each camp believes in a different teaching approach. Parents and teachers are often caught in the middle of these two camps and find it difficult to choose what is most effective. Singapore's situation is the complete opposite; there is a clear, uniform national mathematics curriculum that is integrated from kindergarten up to university levels. In addition, the mathematics curriculum is also connected to other subjects to make up a cohesive K-12 education system that is implemented in every school.

At this point, you may be wondering why the differences between the two countries pose such a challenge to SG Math implementation in the U.S. Let me give you an example. Many parents and educators I've talked to in the U.S. inform me that the reason why they chose to use Singapore's curriculum is because it emphasizes conceptual understanding over computational skills. This line of reasoning reflects a general American attitude towards math education – that it has to be either conceptual or computational. However, the way in which the instructional materials are designed and the teachers are trained in Singapore is based upon a both-and approach; Singaporeans believe that in order to do well in math, children must have *both* conceptual understanding and the ability to compute answers accurately. Because of this disparity in attitude, many American children using SG Math do not get the benefit of having a balance of concepts and calculations. In other words, even though American children may be using the same instructional materials as Singaporean children, they are not learning math in the same way.

PROBLEM 2
There is a lack of information about SG Math in the U.S.

Many parents and educators in the U.S. and around the world took notice of SG Math and began to adopt it when its students topped the ranks of TIMSS and PISA. However, as we have seen in Problem 1, when a curriculum is lifted out of context, it needs to be understood as an element embedded in a broader cultural and socio-political system. Unfortunately, SG Math is often analyzed solely on its instructional materials and theoretical basis in the U.S. This lack of contextual analysis on SG Math not only gives rise to myths and inaccurate representations of the curriculum, it also overlooks many lessons that Singapore has learned over the years, which can prove to be very beneficial when it comes to figuring out the practical applications of a curriculum.

As a doctoral student in math education, I rely heavily on academic texts and research to deepen my knowledge and understanding of the field. On the subject of SG Math, however, I have yet to find studies by U.S. scholars that demonstrate a true understanding of the curriculum. Granted, the pool of research on SG Math is small, but there have been some high-profile papers published. I am going to use the 2005 AIR report[41] as an example to illustrate my point.

The 2005 AIR report is prepared for the U.S. Department of Education and outlines what the U.S. and Singapore math education systems can learn from each other. This 200-page-long document is one of the first official, and most established, academic texts written on SG Math in the U.S. The analysis follows a comparative approach and focuses on four major components of mathematics education – curriculum frameworks, textbooks, assessments, and teachers. Even though the goal of this report is to compare specific features of each country's math education system, it would have been a much stronger report if there were some analysis on how cultural and social differences impact math education as well. There are occasional glimpses of societal differences noted in the report, but there was a clear assumption that these sociological factors do not play as crucial of a role as each of the components discussed.

In addition, despite detailing crucial comparisons between the two country's math education systems, it is concerning that there are no references to any academic articles originating from Singapore in the document. The only Singaporean sources cited are speeches made by politicians and official documents obtained from MOE. Although these sources depict an official account of Singapore's curriculum, they are insufficient to portray a full picture of the local math education landscape. By not citing any Singaporean research on the local curriculum, the AIR report omitted many important components of Singapore's curriculum that set it apart and missed the opportunity to discuss how the curriculum works in reality.

This point about citing Singaporean research in the field of SG Math is critical. As mentioned in the introduction of this book, the field of education cannot exist as a solely theoretical one. It requires practical experiences, field observations, and immersion. If we were to study SG Math based on research that originates from elsewhere, we would never be able to get a full picture of the curriculum because non-Singaporean researchers do not have the cultural knowledge and lived experiences to understand its nuances beyond the theoretical level.

As a result of surface-level research and the lack of knowledge of how the curriculum is taught, SG Math is left open to interpretation in the U.S. Even if parents and educators in the U.S. are teaching the curriculum by the book, they may not be aware of the implicit assumptions embedded within the text and hence unable to capitalize on the curriculum. This is also exactly why there are several myths about SG Math in circulation and how the takeaways I deem so fundamental to the curriculum are not known to many, both of which I will discuss in the subsequent chapters.

CHAPTER 3

Myths of SG Math

In Chapter 2, I discussed why the absence of comprehensive and contextual understanding of how SG Math functions in Singapore poses a huge challenge to the adaptation of the curriculum in the U.S. One of the major issues that arises is the circulation of inaccurate information about the SG Math curriculum in the U.S. Over time, these myths have become the only information available to the public, even though they may not be true. This is detrimental to the successful implementation of SG Math because the myths misinform people who are considering the curriculum and misguide those who are already using it. In an attempt to clarify the inaccuracies propagated by some of the major myths surrounding SG Math, I have identified five I want to debunk in this chapter.

MYTH 1
SG Math is not a spiral curriculum

SG Math has often been categorized in the U.S. as a mastery approach, in contrast to the spiral approach widely used in the U.S.[42] There are two points I want to make in this section. The first is that SG Math can be considered as a spiral curriculum, just not in the same way spiral curriculums are conceptualized in the U.S. The second is that Singapore's mastery approach is not really a direct comparison to the American's spiral approach because these two approaches are not mutually exclusive.

SG Math is a vertical spiral curriculum

A spiral curriculum in the U.S. spirals horizontally, i.e. *within* each grade level. A topic is usually broken up into bite-sized lessons and alternated with lessons from other topics throughout the year. For example, children using a horizontal spiral curriculum may learn multiplication of groups of 1 for the first two lessons of the school year. After that, they switch to a completely different topic, such as geometry, for the next two lessons. A month or two later, multiplication is revisited, but this time, they are taught multiplication of groups of 2. Then, in the last few weeks of first grade, they finally learn how to multiply in groups of 3, which concludes the learning goal for the topic of multiplication in the school year.

Singapore's spiral approach, on the other hand, spirals vertically, i.e. *across* grade levels. Similar to the U.S. approach, math topics are broken down into smaller chapters, but instead of alternating them with lessons from different topics throughout the year, these smaller chapters are taught sequentially, in single chunks at any given grade level. As children advance to the next grade, they spiral back to a similar sequence of topics, revisit some of the content taught previously, and build on their existing knowledge to master more advanced concepts. Using a similar example as above, let's consider a group of first-grade children within a vertical spiral curriculum who have a learning goal of multiplication up to groups of 3. Instead of spending six separate lessons throughout the year to master the goal, they are taught multiplication in six consecutive weeks. Once they have completed the topic on multiplication, they will move on to the next topic, where they spend another six weeks. When this group of children advance to second grade, they will briefly revisit multiplication up to groups of 3, then proceed to build on their existing knowledge to learn multiplication up to groups of 10.

I want to make two more points about SG Math being a vertical spiral curriculum. The topic organization in Singapore's curriculum is often thought of as a traditional and unfavorable way of teaching math because it "tends to teach one skill or concept for a certain period of time before moving on to the next topic - never to return,"[43] so children are unable to reinforce learned concepts. The idea that SG Math does not "return" to a topic that was previously taught reflects a superficial understanding of the curriculum. The reality is that SG Math is specifically designed so that students are required to build on the skills and concepts taught in previous topics. Thus, they are constantly reviewing things they have already learned. For example, when children learn how to add within 10 and move on to the topic of money, they are likely going to have to do some addition of money. Once they advance to a topic like fractions, they will be constantly reviewing and deepening their understanding of addition. Now, this is not to say that children will never need to relearn some concepts or have a more comprehensive review during the school year. What I am saying is that whether or not a child needs to relearn or review concepts does not depend on the curriculum; it depends on the child! Review is always beneficial, and it is up to the teacher and/or parent to determine when and how much revision the child needs.

CURRICULUM TOPICS

- WHOLE NUMBERS
- 4 OPERATIONS
- FRACTIONS
- GEOMETRY
- MEASUREMENTS
- DATA ANALYSIS

VERTICAL SPIRAL CURRICULUM

DIFFICULTY PROGRESSION

YEAR 4
YEAR 3
YEAR 2
YEAR 1

HORIZONTAL SPIRAL CURRICULUM

YEAR 3
YEAR 2
YEAR 1

DIFFICULTY PROGRESSION

FIGURE 9
Vertical vs. horizontal spiral curriculum.

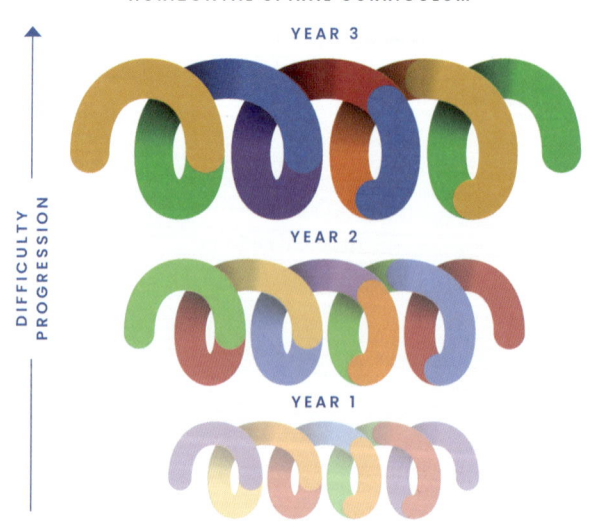

The other point I want to make is in response to the critique that the vertical spiral curriculum of SG Math makes it rigid and inflexible. I have read reviews of parents and educators who believe that SG Math is very inflexible because you stay on a certain topic before moving on to the next. Contrary to common perception in the U.S., teachers in Singapore may not finish all the sub-topics within a chapter. Instead, they often emphasize heavily on the non-negotiables in a particular topic.[44] Non-negotiables are key items that every student needs to know before the teacher moves on to the next topic. Usually, these non-negotiables are planned to support students who need the most help in class. This ensures that no student is left behind in the subsequent topics covered and allows the teacher to build on the concepts throughout the year. This is where the beauty of a vertical spiral curriculum lies. When a struggling student advances to the next grade and encounters a similar topic with more difficulty, they will be more comfortable tackling the topic because of their cognitive development and all the scaffolding they received the previous year. For students who are able to grasp concepts quickly, they can be challenged further within a certain topic beyond the non-negotiable concepts, so that they don't become bored as the teacher wraps up instruction for their peers.

On the flip side, a horizontal spiral curriculum is often thought of as being more flexible because lessons are organized in a less structured way. Such a curriculum reteaches concepts throughout the year because it assumes students simply require repetition to understand difficult concepts. Moreover, because the lessons are bite-sized, all the information in a single lesson are considered non-negotiable skills and concepts, which means that all students are expected to master the same amount of knowledge at each grade level. This makes differentiation in a classroom very challenging because students who work at a slower pace do not have the leniency to spend more time on certain concepts. Meanwhile, students who grasp concepts more quickly will become disengaged when their instructor reteaches a topic for the fourth time that year.

SG Math is a mastery approach

This vertical spiral approach I described above is the way in which many Americans have come to understand SG Math as a mastery approach. This understanding of mastery approach is based on the *organization* of the topics in every grade level, and not what the mastery approach is really about, which brings me to my point that comparing a spiral curriculum with a mastery one is like comparing apples to oranges. In the case of SG Math, it is both a spiral and mastery curriculum.

A mastery approach used in SG Math does not necessarily pertain to the organization of math topics; it encompasses the different components and learning environments that need to exist for children to master a subject. In fact, it is based on Bloom's 1968 research paper[45] on how to learn for mastery. Bloom outlines the variables for mastery learning strategies and shares some of the preconditions, operating procedures, and outcomes of these strategies that were being studied at University of Chicago. These strategies include cultivating perseverance in learners, developing clear and simple instructional materials, and ensuring quality of instruction, all of which are components that curriculum designers in Singapore have incorporated throughout different areas of the curriculum. The goal of using Bloom's mastery approach is not just to improve students' test scores and competencies in a certain subject, but also to formulate a child's self-conceptualization process so that they can develop a positive relationship with the subject.

A good curriculum cannot be defined by just one approach or a singular component. SG Math incorporates mastery strategies, such as developing quality teaching and instructional materials into the organizational structure of math topics for each grade level and across the elementary math system. While it may be beneficial to point out the difference between how topics are organized in SG Math and other American math curricula, it does more harm than good to use an inaccurate term for Singapore's approach in its topic organization. Not only does the inaccuracy in language prevent people from understanding SG Math as a vertical spiral curriculum, it also obfuscates the theoretical underpinnings of Singapore's mastery approach.

MYTH 2
I must buy manipulatives to use SG Math

Many homeschool reviews of SG Math point out that manipulatives are a pricey but essential component of the curriculum. School teachers with minimal budgets have also brought up a similar concern. While manipulatives are very important in SG Math and in teaching children mathematics in general, they need not, and should not, break the bank. If you can spare $50-$60 every year to buy your child or student a grade-specific manipulatives set, I would not advise against it. However, if you are trying to stick to a budget, you can still use SG Math without splurging on colorful counters and blocks.

In order to figure out an alternative to the manipulatives sets on the market, we need to first understand what manipulatives are. Manipulatives are concrete objects that children can manipulate with their hands to better understand abstract concepts through visual, hands-on learning. Because many mathematical concepts are very abstract, manipulatives make math more tangible, especially to young children. The good news is that there are no set criteria for what constitutes a manipulative, so you can literally use anything and everything.

Instead of using counters to teach children addition and subtraction, you can use a pack of M&M's and achieve the same results. One potential scenario could be children counting the total number of M&M's they take out of a packet. Another scenario could be sorting the chocolate pieces into different colors and counting how many M&M's there are in each color. There are endless scenarios you can come up with, and you can do this for 5-10 minutes every day. If you don't want to use M&M's, you can also use paper cups, pencils, pens, cookies, books - whatever you can get your hands on. For me, the best part about using something edible is that you both get a treat after doing math!

Manipulatives sets specific to SG Math often include magnetic strips of different lengths for children to piece out bar models. If you find it hard to keep track of these strips neatly, you can easily simulate bar models without the magnetic strips. You can use pieces of paper that you are already planning to recycle and cut out equal pieces of rectangular strips from them. You can even make the rectangular strips with your child and turn craft time into a math lesson! An added bonus for including the child is that you can teach them how to measure out equal lengths using a ruler and how to divide a piece of paper up into multiple strips.

That is a lesson on division, multiplication, and measurement all in one.

The benefit of not buying a standard manipulatives set is that you get to be creative and bond with your child or student. To be honest, I do not really remember using manipulatives during math lessons in school, even though I went through the "authentic" SG Math. What I do remember, however, is my mom incorporating math into our everyday life. When I was little, my mom would have me count each step as we walked up to our apartment so that I would not complain about getting tired. As my brother and I grew older, my mom would take us with her when she went grocery shopping. Sometimes, she would ask us to total up the cost of the items in our cart. Other times, she would ask us to look at unit cost and help her decide which brand of flour she should buy. As a teacher, I sometimes ask a student to help me take attendance in class by doing a head count, or I'll have them tally up their own scores in a game or on a quiz. Engaging your child or student with math in your everyday life not only improves their math skills but also shows them how practical math is. Even today, I still use many strategies my mom taught me through her shopping trips, such as looking at the unit cost of an item or quickly estimating how much a discounted item costs.

The most important thing to keep in mind as you are using manipulatives is that these concrete objects are here to facilitate children's transition to the pictorial and abstract stage. Let me give you an example. When children are first introduced to the concept of addition, they are likely to grasp it more quickly when they play with counters or actual objects. Through the act of compiling objects, they begin to understand that the total number of objects will increase when you add each one to the pile. Once children reach this understanding, it is time to move on to adding the number of objects they see in a diagram. The ultimate stage is the abstract stage. This is when children deepen their conceptual understanding by recognizing patterns in addition and eventually are able to generalize the process of adding two numbers together.

The true test of conceptual understanding is not whether a child can complete all the problems taught in a lesson, but whether they can apply it in a different context. In the case of addition, a child has only truly understood the concept of addition if they can reason how to add 30 to 40 when they are only taught how to add 10 to 10. Do not fret if they are unable to apply it yet – the learning process takes time! But at that point in their learning, there may not be much value in using manipulatives. Teaching children how to add bigger numbers together does not require them to count the total number of items in a 70-object pile. Instead, work on their pattern recognition, generalization, and reasoning skills because these are the components that will prepare them for advanced learning.

MYTH 3
I have to follow exactly the structure of all instructional materials

Singapore's textbooks and workbooks are intentionally designed with simple graphics and concise wording, so you may find it very easy to teach from them directly. However, the advantage of using SG Math in the U.S. is that you are not restricted by MOE, which means that you do not have to follow the instructional materials as strictly as Singaporean teachers do. The textbooks are a guideline on the flow of the topics and the content teachers should cover in a specific grade level. My teachers rarely required us to follow along in class with our textbooks; they would often print out their own materials or reorganize some topics according to classroom dynamics and their teaching style.

My point is that it is really up to the instructor on how the contents of the textbook are taught. You can rearrange the topics as you see fit. If you see any worthwhile connections between topics, introduce them in class. You can even table some topics in the textbook if you need to spend some time covering concepts required by state standards. While I am a strong advocate for the organization of topics in Singapore's curriculum, all the basic mathematical concepts taught in elementary school do not vary that much between countries, or even between generations. A good mathematics education boils down to *how* you teach the content as much as, or perhaps even more than, the curriculum you use. No matter which math curriculum you end up choosing, remind yourself that they are all just guides, not prescriptions of how you have to teach. That being said, however, I do want to make an argument about the importance of arranging topics in a logical and coherent manner, a point I will discuss in detail in Takeaway 2 in the next chapter. The connections you make from one topic to the next are crucial in helping a child transition and see the relationships between two topics. This is how we can develop children's inter-conceptual connections so that they are able to conceptualize math as an integrated field, instead of one made up of disparate topics.

The workbooks that come with SG Math can also offer a lot of flexibility. You do not have to assign practice questions only when you reach a certain exercise page. You can always choose questions from the workbooks or textbooks that align with your child's or student's needs. If a child requires daily review, then split up a page of exercises into a few different sections so that they can get the practice they need. When they need to review certain concepts, pick out a couple of questions from the topics that they are unsure of and refresh their memory. It does not matter if they have done a question before, especially when they are struggling or have forgotten a concept they have learned previously. Chances are, they probably do not remember that problem they attempted weeks before. To keep children engaged, pick out a variety of questions for them to practice as homework. These are all the strategies that my math teachers in Singapore used so that our homework challenged us and gave us opportunities to synthesize different concepts.

MYTH 4

The Model Method is the only way to solve problems in SG Math

Many people associate bar models with SG Math, and rightfully so! The Model Method is unique to Singapore's curriculum and a central approach to elementary math education in Singapore. However, this is not the only method taught in Singapore. Some American educators who specialize in SG Math encourage using bar models for every word problem. It is certainly possible to use bar models in every situation, but it may not always be the most effective method. In Singapore, teachers impart many other heuristics (or problem-solving strategies) to their students, including guess and check, making a systematic list, simplifying the problem, working backwards, etc. Instead of discounting the guess and check method as haphazard,[46] Singaporean teachers embrace it as one of the problem-solving tools that can be very effective in certain scenarios. The idea is to provide students with as many tools as possible so that they have the ability to choose the most appropriate one for a specific problem. This way, students are also open to the idea that there is more than one way to solve a problem.

This does not mean that students get to pick and choose which heuristic to master and use it on all problems. I've met some students who were taught many different strategies but were told by their teachers to choose one that they can fluently use in all situations. Like the Model Method, different heuristics are useful in different scenarios; unfortunately, there is no one-size-fits-all solution in math. The goal of teaching many different methods is for every student to understand each tool and to be able to choose and execute the best solution in a given situation. When students master all the different ways to solve problems, they can be more flexible in their processes and confidently apply different tools before giving up on the problem. It is imperative that students not focus all their effort on mastering one particular heuristic but instead aim to be fluent in a variety of them.

MYTH 5
SG Math looks so simple that children can learn it on their own

Absolutely not! SG Math is **NOT** designed for children to learn mathematics by themselves. In fact, no math curriculum should be designed that way. Mathematics education develops many important skills and knowledge that we can apply to other areas of our lives. The process of learning mathematics is similar to playing a musical instrument, or picking up a sport, or learning a foreign language. Mastering any one of these requires not only practice but, more importantly, quality instruction.

Singapore's curriculum is designed for use in local schools and is executed by highly trained teachers. The instructional materials, complete with concise wording and colorful graphics, may seem easy to understand, but these explanations and basic concepts are deceptively simple, especially to adults. You may have flipped through a SG Math textbook and wished you had been taught this way, but bear in mind that you are looking at the explanations and solutions through an adult perspective. What may seem like common sense to you is likely the result of decades of math learning and application. To a 7-year-old, the part-whole concept that a bar model can represent is entirely new. Using bar models to solve word problems may be instinctive to me now, but when I was learning it in first grade, it didn't make much sense to me. It took me years of practice and instruction to master the Model Method and many other mathematical skills and concepts. I encourage you to try examining any instructional materials from your child or student's perspective, and be sensitive to their reactions during your teaching. This is something that is easier said than done, but it will transform their educational experience in math and how you teach the subject to them.

Now, don't get me wrong - I'm not saying that a child cannot and should not explore and learn certain concepts and skills on their own. Children should absolutely be nurtured in a way that enables them to think about and do mathematics intuitively. Watching math videos online or reading a math storybook are wonderful *enrichment* tools to help children strengthen what they have learned and stay engaged with their math skill development. Enrichment, however, should not replace guided instruction in your child's chosen curriculum because adult supervision allows opportunities for, what Bruner calls, scaffolding. Bruner argues that scaffolding through interactions and instructional support invites parents and teachers to be active participants in child development.[47] In addition, the act of scaffolding allows children to tap into what Russian development theorist, Lev Vygotsky, refers to as the zone of proximal development (ZPD). When a child can perform a task with the assistance of others but not yet independently, they are within ZPD. As Vygotsky famously stated, "what a child can do with assistance today, she will be able to do by herself tomorrow."[48] Vygotsky's theory of ZPD and his emphasis on the role of social environments in child development speak to the importance of interactions in the process of learning. When children attempt to learn mathematics on their own, they lose out on the opportunities to develop skills in their ZPD and to learn how to communicate mathematical ideas and reasoning verbally.

FIGURE 10 ▼

Vygotsky's model of the zone of proximal development[49]

ZONE OF PROXIMAL DEVELOPMENT

A: Stuff learners can do.
ZPD: Stuff learners can do, with support.
B: Stuff learners can't do (even with support).

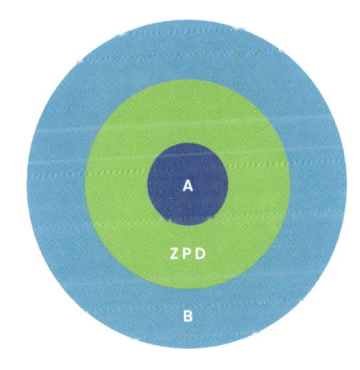

CHAPTER 4
The Real Takeaways of SG Math

According to one online article on the74million.com[50], there are six reasons why SG Math is superior to other curricula in the U.S. The reasons listed are:

1. Singapore students rank at the top for TIMSS and PISA

2. SG Math focuses on mastery, covering fewer topics a year

3. Visual and concrete representations are key in the curriculum

4. Topics build on one another in a vertical spiral approach

5. Many editions of SG Math instructional materials align with Common Core standards

6. Research has shown students improve in their math abilities after using the curriculum

While the points made above are valid, they only provide a superficial side of the story. This is why parents and educators are misled into thinking that if they follow the instructional materials and adopt the most popular features of the curriculum, their children and students will be able to achieve at the same level as their Singaporean peers in mathematics. Unfortunately, many who have implemented SG Math are disappointed by the results, which is likely due to the misrepresentations of SG Math, perpetuation of myths, and a lack of in-depth analysis beyond the theoretical level.

You will see below that I have summarized eight takeaways that most people rarely discuss about SG Math but are essential to successfully implementing the curriculum. These takeaways are my reflections and observations of the education system and society I grew up in, which might provide an alternative explanation for why the curriculum works and why Singaporean students do so well in math.

TAKEAWAY 1
Invest in elementary mathematics education

As I have mentioned in Chapter 2, education is the cornerstone of Singapore's society. Quality elementary and STEM education have always been Singapore's two major priorities since its independence in 1965. Due to a lack of natural resources, Singapore recognized from the beginning the importance of effectively educating its people. Providing free universal elementary education successfully raised literacy rates, while an emphasis on STEM prepared manpower for Singapore's economic strategies. Today, with an adult literacy rate of 97.3%[51] and an impressive GDP of US$364.2 billion[52], Singapore continues to invest heavily in education.

While Singapore initially focused on STEM education to support the manufacturing sector, its leaders quickly recognized that nurturing STEM talents at a young age would be fundamental to the country's progress. Since mathematics is at the core of all other STEM subjects, Singapore has devoted many resources to research and fine-tune its elementary mathematics education. This allows Singapore to create a wider pipeline of talented students who would grow up to become not just mathematicians but also engineers, research scientists, data analysts, and other STEM professionals. Graduates of the program would also bring a high level of data literacy into their careers.

Elementary math education builds the foundation for middle and high school success

In the U.S., there have been major efforts to improve high school math programs, starting with former President George W. Bush's proposal to train more high school teachers to lead AP courses in math and science. However, as Barry Garelick pointed out in his Education Next article, "the success of high-school students in math depends on what they've learned in lower grades."[53] Garelick is absolutely spot-on in his comment. Elementary mathematics education paves the way for success in high school math. A professor emeritus of mathematics at UC Berkeley, Hung-Hsi Wu, argues that the "simple" concepts we associate with elementary mathematics, such as adding two whole numbers, may not be as simple as we think.[54] Wu contends that the skillful teaching of basic concepts must include the development of children's ability to argue with "coherence, precision and reasoning,"[55] which is fundamental to learning mathematics.

Without a solid foundation in basic concepts, children are going to find it difficult to keep up with middle and high school mathematics, which is when the subject becomes increasingly abstract and requires them to build on previously-taught concepts. In my personal experience, it is difficult to teach middle grade students Algebra 1 when they lack an understanding of elementary concepts and skills. Teaching math to middle school or high school students with a poor foundation is like fixing a plane while flying it - you have to patch up the holes where there are missing skills or concepts, but at the same time, you have to make sure that new material is taught so that they don't fall behind their grade level.

The responsibility of building a successful early mathematics education does not fall solely on schools and educators. Parents and caregivers play a crucial part in making sure that their child's foundation is solid. Speaking from my own experience, my mom made a huge difference in my elementary mathematics education. She spent a lot of time and effort reviewing test papers with me and reteaching concepts I was unsure about until I mastered the basics. Even with the time and effort my mom spent with me, I was mediocre in math throughout my elementary school years. I have also most certainly thrown my fair share of tantrums when I didn't want to work on math anymore.

However, everything clicked in place for me once I started middle school. I had no problems understanding abstract concepts and was more than fluent in manipulating algebraic expressions. Soon enough, I was able to study on my own and excelled in math in middle and high school. My mom rarely had to help me in math after elementary school. Years later, she told me that she wanted to make sure I had a solid understanding in elementary school math so that I could develop more advanced skills and concepts more easily in the future, just like how a stable structural foundation is important for a building.

Elementary math education can help develop children's intuition about mathematics

This next point I want to discuss is something that rarely appears in the discussions of mathematics education, especially in the elementary stage. When I was learning Spanish a few years ago, my teacher told the adult class that even if we manage to become fluent in Spanish now, we will never be able to feel the language like native speakers because we cannot intuit the nuances of the language. Some people in the class were clearly offended, but I was not. I completely understood what he was talking about.

As an educator, I believe that the age someone learns a new language or skill doesn't matter, but there is something to be said about learning certain skills at an early age. I grew up speaking English and Mandarin Chinese at the same time because English is the primary language of instruction in Singapore, and Mandarin Chinese is my mother tongue. After spending most of my life communicating in English, speaking Chinese feels slightly foreign. But even so, I can tell immediately when someone is not a native Chinese speaker or when something just does not sound right. I may not be able to tell you why or how I know, but I have a certain intuition about the language that I have developed over the years from exposure to native speakers at home.

The intuition we all have towards languages is also applicable to the field of mathematics. Children can develop an affinity for and sensitivity towards numbers and mathematical concepts when they build a strong foundation in elementary school. These intuitive sentiments can be very helpful in advanced math classes because students will be able to tell if an answer looks wrong or if they are going down a rabbit hole when solving a problem. In professional workplaces, an astute understanding of data is an effective tool for spotting mistakes and pinpointing the root causes of an issue. Most importantly, nurturing mathematical instincts in the next generation of educators will allow them to be more conscious of common errors in students' calculations or processes.

It is important to keep in mind that the ability to develop an intuition for mathematics does not belong to "geniuses" or to individuals who supposedly have the "math gene." Educational psychologists believe that children are programmed by nature to learn about numbers. Research has shown that babies show a sensitivity to the quantity of things and to concepts like "more than" and "less than."[56] This means that children are armed with an innate sense of equivalence and relative quantity when they enter school. Like language, mathematics has its own set of rules and specific ways to communicate an idea, and children are taught the mathematical language in school.

A good elementary mathematics curriculum does not assume that children are blank slates but should instead build on what children already know intuitively and teach them the structure and rules of mathematics simultaneously. When children do not receive quality mathematics instruction at a young age, they may miss out on key developmental stages that contribute to an intuitive understanding of the concepts.

Elementary math education expands children's educational and career opportunities

When we build a strong foundation and develop children's intuition in math, we are setting them up for success not only in advanced mathematics courses, but in life as well. Whether we like it or not, standardized testing has determined the educational and career paths for many people, and mathematics is a core component of any high-stakes testing. It is imperative that we realize that mathematics is an important gatekeeper in children's lives. Even as colleges across the nation are opting for test-optional processes, students' GPA and the courses they take in high school will still be a huge consideration factor for college admissions, major requirements, and eligibility for merit scholarships.

In the last couple of decades, STEM careers have exponentially increased. According to the U.S. Bureau of Labor Statistics, there were 8.6 million STEM jobs in 2015, which make up about 6.2% of total U.S. employment. The number of STEM jobs has grown 79% since 1990 and is consistently outpacing overall U.S. job growth.[57] STEM workers also tend to earn more than similarly educated non-STEM workers, with the national average wage for all STEM occupations being $87,570, nearly double the national average wage for non-STEM occupations at $45,700.[58]

Giving children the opportunity to consider a STEM career does not and should not start in high school, or even college, because it could be too late for them to take AP classes or meet additional requirements. As I have mentioned in previous sections, success in middle and high school mathematics begins at the elementary level. This means that if we do not provide quality mathematics instruction to elementary school children, we are doing them a disservice by closing many doors in STEM before they can make their own decision.

STEM workers tend to earn more than similarly educated non-STEM workers

Median annual earnings of full-time, year-round workers ages 25 and older with positive earnings

Among those who work in...
- STEM Jobs
- Non-STEM Jobs

Education	STEM	Non-STEM
High school or less	$45,569	$33,000
Some college	$54,745	$40,505
Bachelor's degree	$75,948	$55,695
Master's degree	$91,137	$67,847
Professional/doctoral degree	$120,000	$91,242

Note: Figures based on 2016 dollars. Some college includes those with an associate degree and those who attended college but did not obtain a degree. Professional degree includes those with an M.D., DDS, DVM, LL B. or J.D. Doctoral degree includes those with a Ph.D. or Ed.D. STEM stands for science, technology, engineering and math.

Source: Pew Research Center analysis of 2014-2016 American Community Survey (IPUMS). "Women and Men in STEM Often at Odds Over Workplace Equity"

FIGURE 11 ▲

Salaries of STEM vs. non-STEM workers, Source: Pew Research Center[59]

FIGURE 12 ▼

Recent and projected STEM and non-STEM employment growth, Source: Bureau of Labor Statistics[60]

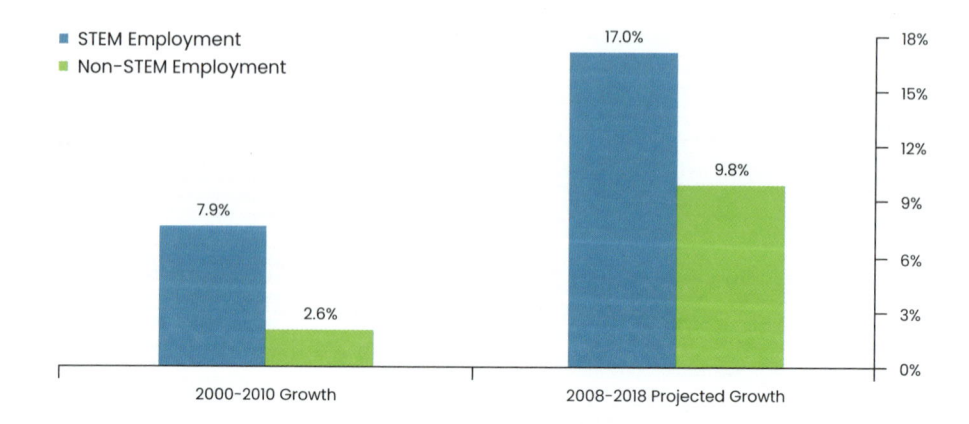

- STEM Employment
- Non-STEM Employment

Period	STEM	Non-STEM
2000-2010 Growth	7.9%	2.6%
2008-2018 Projected Growth	17.0%	9.8%

The benefits of studying mathematics are not just about high-paying career prospects. Even if children turn out to be interested in non-STEM subjects, their mathematical abilities such as critical thinking skills, logic, and data literacy will be relevant and applicable to many situations and careers. We have all heard that mathematics stimulates the left side of our brains while humanities and the arts occupy the right. But both sides of our brains complement each other. As a double major in mathematics and art history, I have come across many people who think that my areas of study are contradictory, but in reality, they work perfectly together. The ability to think logically and construct coherent proofs allowed me to write compelling arguments in my art history papers. On the other hand, the process of understanding the historical context of art pieces inspires me to look beyond the numbers in math and visualize what the numbers represent.

In the last section, I talked about the development of mathematical intuition, but I did not discuss how it can cultivate arguably one of the most important skills in today's world - data literacy. Big data is bigger than ever before, which means that data literacy is increasingly important. Data literacy refers to the ability to analyze, interpret, and communicate data and data sources, but I argue that data literacy is so much more than charting graphs and creating reports. At the heart of data literacy is the responsibility to *humanize* data. It is the responsibility of individuals to tell stories about the data presented in front of them and to recognize the biases of the creators behind computers and regression models. The ability to recognize discrepancies within statistics or trends boils down to an intuition for the structures, algorithms, and numbers of mathematics. That intuition can be sharpened by a good foundation in math and years of mathematical training and contribute to cultivating the responsible and ethical usage of data in every industry.

TAKEAWAY 2
A logically and coherently structured mathematics curriculum is key

When I first started out in education, I was convinced that a horizontally spiraled curriculum is the way to go. In theory, this kind of approach makes a lot of sense: children can easily forget what they learn at the beginning of the year if concepts and skills don't get revisited periodically, so we should alternate lessons from different topics throughout the year. However, after I started teaching students who were using a horizontal spiral curriculum, I realized that the implementation of this approach may not be as enticing as its theory.

Breaking up mathematical topics into bite-sized lessons is a great idea, but the flow of the lessons has to be logical and coherent, which, unfortunately, is not how most of these horizontally spiraled curricula are structured. When the lessons are not organized in relation with one another, mathematics is presented as an inherently disjointed discipline, in which different topics are non-intersecting and exist as independent concepts. Incoherent lessons are not just confusing to both students and teachers, they also require everyone to put in more work.

Let us consider a second-grade lesson structure for a popular, horizontal spiral curriculum among homeschool families that I have taught. The first lesson contains the identification of numbers up to 100 and the spatial recognition of left and right. The curriculum seems like it is off to a great start – instructors can establish a link between numbers and directions by introducing the concept of a number line. This way, children not only learn how to identify numbers but also recognize that every number is positioned in relation to another, which lays the foundation for positive and negative numbers. However, in the second lesson, while children continue to build on some of the concepts learned in the first lesson to understand basic addition and subtraction, data graphing is abruptly introduced and does not make a reappearance until lesson 16. Lesson 3 moves away completely from whole numbers and covers the topic of time. The rest of the curriculum follows the pattern of the first three lessons, jumping around from one topic to the next with no underlying logic connecting these lessons together. While the length of each lesson may be manageable for children to go through daily, the lessons on the whole form an incoherent curriculum.

In comparison, SG Math is a highly logical and coherent curriculum. In the U.S. edition of *Primary Mathematics* 2A textbook, there are six major chapters: Numbers to 1000, Addition and Subtraction, Length, Weight, Multiplication and Division, and Multiplication Tables of 2 and 3. Within a certain chapter, lessons are introduced systematically. For example, in the Length chapter, children first learn how to measure length in meters, then centimeters, followed by yards and feet, and finally, in inches. There is also a connection across chapters. When children learn length and weight in Chapters 3 and 4, they are synthesizing what they have learned in whole numbers (in Chapter 1) with the concept of having a measurement unit to group like-terms together (introduced in Chapter 2).

When individual lessons do not serve to build up children's knowledge systematically, it is going to be challenging for them to grasp more advanced concepts. In the same second-grade horizontal curriculum I described above, children are introduced to the concept of division by dividing a whole into halves, fourths, and eighths. One hundred lessons later, children are taught how to divide by two. As adults, we may think that dividing a whole into halves is similar to dividing by two, but these two concepts are drastically different. In order to understand how to divide one whole into different pieces, children are essentially learning fractions. It is much easier, however, to divide eight candies among two children and to demonstrate that division is the opposite of multiplication. However, as we see in SG Math example above, children are first introduced to the concept of multiplication and division by grouping things together, and only then are they introduced to multiplication tables of 2 and 3. A logical curriculum has to take into account the order of learning because it matters in how teachers can scaffold children's conceptual understanding and gradually prepare them for more abstract topics.

Moreover, having an incoherent curriculum requires children and teachers to do more work. When teachers use a disjointed curriculum, half of their job is trying to figure out how to make connections between each lesson and create a structured mathematical framework for their students. It is important to note that children do not only learn mathematics through the content of their instructional materials but also through the structure of the curriculum and the logic behind procedures. When a curriculum transitions nicely from one lesson to another and sets up many connections between the concepts, children are guided to think in a more logical and coherent way and will be able to organize their notes and thoughts systematically.

Madge Goldman, the president of the Rosenbaum foundation that helped to arrange the *Primary Mathematics* series for the American system, has aptly recognized in her preface to the teacher's guide of the U.S. edition that "understanding the structure of mathematics is the key to success."[61] Bill Gates has also argued that having a structure or a framework is extremely important in learning and recalling information. In a piece titled "Training your brain for recall," Gates writes that he does not have a photographic memory. He does mention, however, that for the domains he spends a lot of time thinking about, he has "a structure or a context that the facts can fit into."[62]

When you look at SG Math textbooks, the topics and chapters are laid out in a very structured way, which provides the framework for students and teachers to organize concepts. This makes it much easier for teachers to link mathematical concepts together and for children to develop strong inter- and intra-conceptual understanding.

For example, the topic of area and perimeter in a *Primary Mathematics* textbook is systematically broken down into smaller lessons. Children first learn about the concepts of area and perimeter in rectangles and squares and then move on to learn how to find the area and perimeter of composite figures. When children are introduced to the topic of area and perimeter systematically, they will associate the terms "length" and "width" with the topic and master the concepts of both area and perimeter. Furthermore, instructors can use this opportunity to let the child observe and note the differences between a rectangle and a square. By clearly organizing the lessons of perimeter, area, length, and width under the broader topic of area and perimeter, SG Math has created a structural framework that saves children and teachers the time and effort that they would need to reorganize their notes and make connections themselves.

On the other hand, I have met many students using a horizontal spiral curriculum who are unable to explain what they have learned in a single lesson in connection with all the other concepts they have learned previously. Using the same topic of area and perimeter as above, a horizontal curriculum would introduce the length and width of a rectangle in lesson 6. In lesson 49, children are taught the concept of perimeter, and only in lesson 108 is the concept of area introduced. That's 40-60 different lessons in between each of these concepts within the topic of area and perimeter. This means that by the time the child is learning how to calculate the area of a rectangle, they have to remember what length and width are from lesson 6 and integrate those concepts with their multiplication and addition skills.

Occasionally, I meet a student who is able to connect lessons 49 and 108 with lesson 6 and classify these three lessons under the broader topic of area and perimeter, or even geometry. However, the majority of students who come to me for help struggle in figuring out which concepts to apply or how to use different concepts they have learned in tandem with each other. More often than not, I have to create a structural framework for the students by myself. I would either make connections between previous concepts with the current lessons when I have to review and reteach content, or I would re-organize all the lessons before I start teaching. So, while it may seem like a good idea to engage a child with the constant introduction of new topics, the lack of structure and connections between lessons may prove to be more detrimental than beneficial to children's learning and long-term skill development.

TAKEAWAY 3
Emphasize problem-solving processes

Processes are a key component of the SG Math framework but often get overlooked when the curriculum travels outside of Singapore. Many of us also tend to use mathematical processes and procedures interchangeably because we show our thinking process by writing down the appropriate steps and procedures to get to a mathematical solution. While processes and procedures may look the same on paper, they are two interrelated, yet very different, elements. According to the International Organisation for Standardisation (ISO), processes are "interrelated or interacting activities which transform inputs into outputs," whereas procedures are a specific way to "carry out an activity or a process."[63] The difference between processes and procedures in the context of math is illustrated in Figure 13.

FIGURE 13
Processes vs. procedures

Question: 100 − 8 = ?

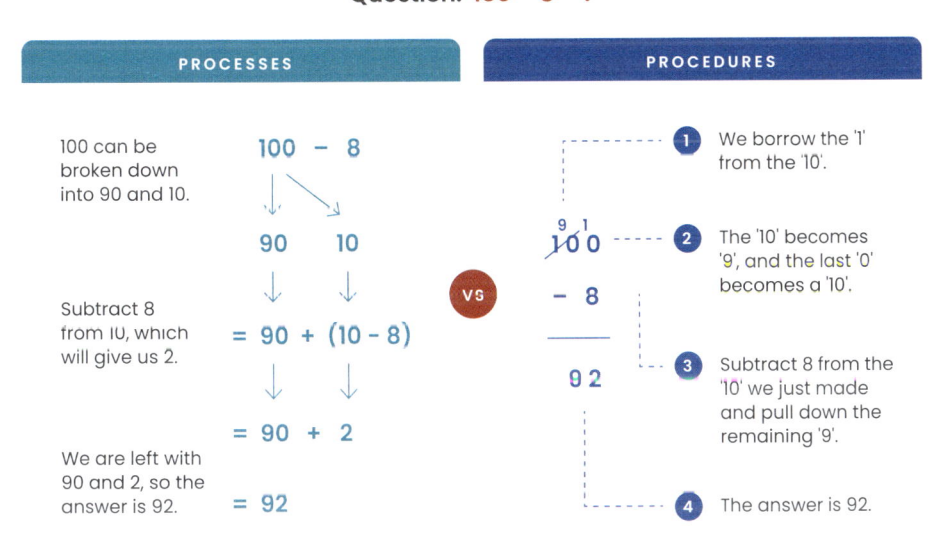

PROCESSES		PROCEDURES
100 can be broken down into 90 and 10.	100 − 8 ↓ ↘ 90 10 ↓ ↓	**1** We borrow the '1' from the '10'.
Subtract 8 from 10, which will give us 2.	= 90 + (10 − 8) ↓ ↓	$\overset{9\ 1}{\cancel{10}0}$ − 8 ———— 9 2
		2 The '10' becomes '9', and the last '0' becomes a '10'.
We are left with 90 and 2, so the answer is 92.	= 90 + 2 = 92	**3** Subtract 8 from the '10' we just made and pull down the remaining '9'.
		4 The answer is 92.

VS

As mentioned in Chapter 1, Singapore's curriculum aims to guide children through Pólya's four-step problem-solving process[64]:

1. Understand the problem
2. Devise a plan
3. Carry out the plan
4. Check your answer

There is no need for students to memorize these four steps in Singapore. Instead, teachers ask questions in class to guide them through Pólya's problem-solving framework. This way, students truly understand how to get from one step to the next and the concepts behind each step. The benefit of using Pólya's four steps is that they present an open-ended framework to think through a problem that can be applied to any situation. Students are encouraged to devise their own plan to solve challenges and are not limited to a specific procedure that they have to follow. This is also why Singaporean teachers make it a point to teach their students different heuristics so that they have all the appropriate tools necessary and are encouraged to think outside the box.

This emphasis on processes does not only exist in classrooms - students' mathematical processes are so important that they are integrated into the assessment structure. American assessments are often saturated with multiple-choice questions (MCQs), no matter what grade level students are in. However, in Singapore, MCQs are few and far between, especially when students move up to more advanced grades. This difference in assessment is documented in the 2005 AIR report[65] that describes what the

U.S. can learn from Singapore. Unfortunately, the team of researchers did not mention how teachers assign grades in Singapore. Open-ended and short response questions used in Singapore's assessments allow teachers to give credit for each logical step that students write down. Whereas MCQs are extremely high-stakes – you either get full credit or no credit at all – the Singapore approach awards partial credit for their thought process. In addition, teachers in Singapore have a grading code called "error carry forward," which teachers use to commend a student's problem-solving process when they have carried a careless mistake through in their calculations. Singaporean teachers rarely grade on the final answer; they spend time looking through every step in homework questions and in test papers so that they can direct students' attention to their mistakes. By paying equal and sometimes more attention to mathematical processes, teachers encourage students in Singapore to try the problem and not give up. This helps to cultivate a persevering attitude and confidence to creatively solve problems.

As important as processes are in solving math problems, we cannot neglect the role in which procedures and standard algorithms play in math. Both processes and procedures have to be utilized effectively to solve problems. In the next takeaway, I will elaborate on the importance of procedural competence.

TAKEAWAY 4
Procedures are important, but they do not have to be memorized

As I have noted in Chapter 2, there is a false dichotomy that forces reformists and traditionalists of math education to choose between focusing on conceptual understanding and procedural competence. Some parents and reform educators are understandably fighting for an emphasis on conceptual understanding so that children will not have to memorize procedures blindly. However, neglecting procedural competency while promoting conceptual understanding is not going to improve children's mathematical skills. Children must be expected to be fluent in standard algorithms in math because in doing so, they "can gain insight into the fact that mathematics is well structured (highly organized, filled with patterns, predictable),"[66] just like how a logical flow of topics in math textbooks can demonstrate the coherent nature of math as a discipline. Procedures and conceptual understanding exist in a dialectical relationship, and they have to be delicately balanced in a quality mathematics education. It is certainly true that students who understand the underlying concepts are less likely to make computational and procedural errors, but on the other hand, they also require a certain level of technical skill to deepen their understanding of concepts.

In the previous takeaway, I mentioned that children have to use processes and procedures together to achieve mathematical proficiency. Conceptual understanding is also demonstrated through logical processes and accurate procedures. Singaporean teachers know how to integrate the explanation of processes and procedures with mathematical concepts so that children develop in-depth comprehension of all the components in play. They make sure that the explanation and presentation of heuristics are clear during lessons because these provide the logical scaffolds to help students master concepts and skills in a systematic fashion.[67] Teachers in Singapore explain in detail why a particular heuristic is being used (processes), and they proceed to present how it is used (procedures). The procedural steps that teachers go through with their students aim to show the logical progression between each step and what concepts are applied.

The ways in which teachers in Singapore integrate concepts with processes and procedures are rarely examined in the implementation of SG Math in the U.S. I once came across an eight-step problem-solving plan created by a SG Math expert in the U.S., Bob Hogan.[68] Hogan's plan outlines eight simple steps to employ bar models as a foolproof way to tackle any elementary math word problem. When the plan was adopted by some schools, it required students to memorize the eight steps to solve problems.[69] Not only is it erroneous to assume that bar models are the only way to solve any and every elementary math word problem, but Hogan's plan is also carried out in a problematic way. Instead of guiding children through an open-ended framework like Pólya's, requiring them to memorize eight steps makes bar models and the problem-solving process unengaging, procedural, and mechanical. This adaptation of bar models and SG Math does not constitute good math education.

A good mathematics education must not only include the teaching of concepts, but it has to also show students the nature of mathematics, through the organization of lessons and presentation of how processes and procedures are integrated to solve abstract concepts. When children are presented with a comprehensive view of mathematics and a clear picture of how all the components work together, they will not need to memorize any procedures.

TAKEAWAY 5
Practice, practice, practice!

Not only is it important for children to know which procedures to use and how to use them, they also need to be efficient and accurate in their calculations. When children understand mathematical concepts, but are unable to compute accurately and efficiently, they will be unable to demonstrate their mathematical proficiency and will perform poorly on tests. Accuracy and efficiency are crucial in today's world of high-stakes assessments that are saturated with MCQs. Standardized testing is not an evaluation of who knows the most concepts; it is instead a competition between which child is able to make the fewest mistakes within a given time constraint.

In addition, the lack of computational skills and procedural fluency will impact their ability to perform higher-order thinking skills because "their mental space will be overcrowded in figuring out both problem solving and equation solving."[70] This means that the concentration spent on figuring out computations will significantly obstruct their ability to see important relationships between concepts and develop other instrumental skills. Freeing up mental space for higher-order thinking is also incredibly important in an assessment setting because children *will* encounter questions they are unfamiliar with, and they can use that extra time and mental capacity to solve challenging problems.

This is where practice comes in. While some reviews have pointed out that the instructional materials for Singapore's curriculum in the U.S. do not provide enough practice, that is not the case in Singapore. Practice is a huge deal in Singapore's education landscape in general. Local bookstores are stocked with "assessment books," which are books full of practice questions and review chapters for every school subject. Children in Singapore routinely complete at least one assessment book per subject every grade. To prepare for national examinations, middle and high school students use a ten-year series, which are test papers from the past ten years collated and published in a book. These ten-year series are not only for individual use, but they are also used in schools and by teachers for extra assigned homework.

Obviously, Singapore's case is one of over-practice, but the necessity of practice should be valued more in the U.S. It is important to recognize that practice does *not* equate to drilling; it should not look like endless pages of worksheets with a hundred different variations of the same problem. Instead, practice should include a variety of problems that involve similar and interrelated concepts. Practice improves children's ability to compute accurately and efficiently, as well as apply concepts in a wide variety of contexts. Exposure to different problems strengthens the students' conceptual understanding and, at the same time, provides them the opportunity to decide which procedures to use and how to accurately apply them. Many Americans tend to believe that when children understand the concept, they should be able to apply what they have learned in any given situation. However, teachers in Singapore believe children have to be able to apply a concept in a variety of situations before they have mastered it.

Students in Singapore are exposed to many different types of problems for this exact reason. They practice applying concepts to various scenarios and learn to make connections they may not have thought about at the theoretical level. Furthermore, the exposure to many types of questions prepares students to take on nonroutine problems that they have never seen before. This is a great advantage for them under stressful testing situations because they have a flexible understanding to tackle even the unfamiliar questions.

TAKEAWAY 6
Integrate test-taking techniques in math lessons

In Takeaways 3 through 5, I discussed how children's conceptual understanding and procedural fluency have to be developed together through logical scaffolding and sufficient practice. When students develop a solid understanding of concepts and are fluent in algorithms, they will approach difficult problems with greater confidence. If they are also able to master test-taking strategies and be encouraged to solve nonroutine problems in class, they will be much more confident to face unknown challenges during tests. This takeaway aims to show that test-taking strategies need not be a standalone skill that teachers spend additional time teaching. These strategies can be incorporated in pedagogical tools to support conceptual understanding and computation skills.

Taking a test will always be nerve-wracking, no matter how confident you are in the subject. Mathematics is a gatekeeper to many higher education opportunities because it is a core subject of many high-stakes assessments, so the pressure for children to perform well is a huge burden for both teachers and parents. Standardized testing is not designed to assess how much a child knows; it is a competition of strategies.

This makes test-taking techniques very important and a necessity in many education systems. In Singapore, testing is an integral component of the education system. As a result, teachers in local schools integrate many test-taking strategies into their instructional practice. My teachers used to teach my classmates and me how to identify and categorize the different kinds of questions, analyze the breakdown of topics in test questions, and concentrate on particular topics to maximize our scores. My classmates and I also had to keep an organized folder of all our worksheets and homework as a revision structure for future tests. Although these strategies are not apparent on official curriculum documents, they play a major role in Singaporean teachers' instructional practices.

In the U.S., teaching to the test has a bad connotation. It usually means students are forced to memorize formulae or make effective guesses to get a higher score, instead of learning and mastering concepts. I want to challenge this notion here and argue that test-taking techniques can be useful outside of testing situations. In Singapore, these strategies are often embedded within the curriculum. Remember the famous Model Method? As much as this method is a visualization tool, it is also one that teaches students to be meticulous and detail-oriented in the comprehension of word problems. When children draw out bar models, they are reinterpreting the problem in a visual way. More importantly, they have to pay close attention to the inputs, the output, and the relationships between the inputs and the output of the problem they are trying to solve.[71] In order to draw accurate diagrams, children must process the right information, which means that they have to reference the question constantly and carefully to update their models. This process essentially helps to prevent and minimize careless mistakes made during lessons and especially during tests. Being meticulous is not just a good habit to have for testing, but a great life skill to have.

Another strategy that is more specific to test-taking is how to analyze a test paper. This technique is something I have personally used with great success. I was taught at an early age, by both my mom and teachers, to notice the common topics that appear in a test. Once I knew which topics were bound to be tested, I would focus my reviews on the concepts within those topics. But the more important thing I learned through this process is how to perform data analysis. I had to first sieve through the data, i.e. all the questions on a test paper, and look for patterns. Then I grouped the test questions that fit a similar pattern together and calculated the percentage of occurrence of each topic. So, in a way, I applied the basics of data analysis and probability before I was even taught these concepts in class. The funny thing is that everything that I did when I was seven to analyze a test paper is exactly the same process I went through every day as a professional data analyst. The ability to sort through data and pick out patterns is as much of a test-taking strategy as it is a useful skill in work and daily life.

TAKEAWAY 7
Develop children's mathematical mindsets

With the publishing of Dweck's book on growth mindsets and Boaler's book on mathematical mindsets, mathematics education in the U.S. has been steadily picking up these educational psychology theories. There is ample scholarship[72] that supports the importance of nurturing students to believe in the possibility of improving their mathematical abilities instead of perceiving them as innate.

When children understand that mathematics is a subject that they can excel in if they put in the time and effort, they are more likely to persevere through problems and have the conviction that intellectual growth is possible and not biologically determined.

Singapore's curriculum is clear that it aims to develop students' positive attitude towards mathematics. For decades, Singapore has been creating a learning environment where students are encouraged to work hard and persevere through their studies. It is unfortunate that this component of Singapore's curriculum did not gain traction when it arrived in the U.S. market in the early 2000s. In fact, the attitudes component in Singapore's curriculum framework continues to be an aspect that advocates of SG Math in the U.S. rarely discuss.

One of the main observations I made from teaching mathematics in the U.S. is that many students are hesitant to try problems that they have never seen before. They would agree to read the question and think independently for a couple of minutes and then give up without penning any of their thoughts down. When I nudge them and suggest that they write down key pieces of information from the question, they are able to either identify the right approach or figure out the solution on their own. An important heuristic and pedagogical tool that Singapore's curriculum focuses on is visualization. This cultivates children's habit to draw or write out key information in order to process the problem effectively. It also encourages them to always attempt the question even if they merely copy down the question. When children start to move their pencil, they are breaking the perception that the problem is too daunting to attempt. There is power in attempting an unknown problem and knowing that it is okay to make a mistake.[73] As mentioned in Takeaway 3, Singapore's teachers grade students' work based on the processes shown and not just the final answers. Even though students might be penalized for making calculation mistakes, they know that they are also being evaluated on their reasoning skills, and their mistakes are not the end of the world. This encourages students to always attempt every question they encounter and learn from their mistakes. Once students realize that it is completely within their power to face challenging problems and they are able to solve them, their confidence will rise and so will their positivity towards mathematics.

The 2012 PISA results showed that Singapore's students not only did well on the test questions, but they also demonstrated a high level of perseverance and openness to problem-solving, which were two new scaled indices added that year. When asked if they give up easily when confronted with a problem, 62% of Singaporean students answered no, in contrast to the 56% OECD average.[74] The data also revealed that 61% of Singapore's 15-year-olds are budding perfectionists, as compared to the 44% OECD average.[75] The above-average indices scores are not surprising since Singapore has been cultivating these attitudes and character traits more than a decade before its PISA participation.

TAKEAWAY 8
Commit to a curriculum and be flexible

As the saying goes, Rome was not built in a day. It took Singapore three decades of research and innovation to top international charts in mathematics. This also proves that no matter how great a curriculum is, it takes time for the effects of education to unfold. Even as SG Math is yielding great success, Singapore continues to revise, review, and innovate in mathematics education.

It is very important for parents and educators to commit to a curriculum, no matter which one it is. If Singapore had chosen to switch to a new curriculum every couple of years, its students will not be able to demonstrate such high levels of math achievement. I have read many reviews from homeschool parents who ended up switching to a new curriculum when SG Math reportedly did not work for their children. I have also read reports of schools and districts that implemented SG Math for three years and decided to switch. When educators and parents choose a mathematics curriculum to implement, they need to make an informed decision and understand exactly why they chose it. This way, during implementation, they know which aspects to stick to and which aspects can be tailored to the students.

No math curriculum is suitable for every single child, so parents and educators should always be flexible and make constant tweaks to the curriculum. However, switching to a completely new curriculum after a couple of months or even after one or two years is going to severely disrupt children's learning journey in elementary math. Don't expect to see immediate results when you start a new math curriculum. And just because a child does not respond well to a curriculum at the beginning, it does not mean that the curriculum doesn't work. It takes time for children (and also parents/teachers) to get used to the sequencing of a curriculum and the way information is presented and taught, as well as a lot of effort from parents and teachers to modify the curriculum to suit a child's developmental needs.

It is also crucial to choose a curriculum that is updated and revised regularly, because if it is not, it is not a curriculum worth using. When curriculum designers update the instructional materials or syllabi in Singapore, they confer with teachers and conduct tons of research to make sure that any changes they make align with teachers' instructional practice and are beneficial to the students. A curriculum that is not reviewed and revised does not take into account feedback from teachers or consider new and innovative pedagogical research. Be sure to keep up with the key updates on the curriculum you choose so that the educational materials are not outdated.

CHAPTER 5

How do we implement SG Math more effectively in the U.S.?

In Chapter 2, I identified two major problems in the implementation of SG Math in the U.S. The first problem I discussed is the lack of consideration for the socio-cultural differences between Singaporean and American society. Because of this, SG Math is analyzed in an inaccurate context, which results in a multitude of interpretations and adaptations of the curriculum in the U.S. The second problem I pointed out is the lack of research materials on SG Math from Singapore in circulation in the U.S. This problem affects the quality of information about SG Math, as well as Americans' understanding of the curriculum. Both of these problems contribute to myths and misrepresentations of SG Math in the U.S.

By presenting SG Math as an individual who has gone through it as a student in Singapore, I hope to rectify some of the misrepresentations about the curriculum. In this last chapter, I want to synthesize the myths and takeaways discussed in previous chapters and provide some actionable items for parents and educators to implement SG Math more effectively.

ACTION ITEM 1
Do more research

I know this is a big ask because we all have a lot of things on our plate. It is challenging enough for us to take the time to read recreationally or have a hobby, much less do research on Singapore's math curriculum. But all I am asking here is for you to go beyond the news articles and the homeschool blogposts and skim through a handful of research papers written by Singaporean academics. I have made it a point to include scholarship originating from Singapore in this book that examines the history, theoretical underpinnings, and the implementation of SG Math curriculum locally, with a full bibliography attached. The good news is that most of them can be accessed for free through the Google Scholar platform. Browsing some local perspectives will not only deepen your understanding of the curriculum, it will also give you ideas on how to implement SG Math in your classroom or at home.

ACTION ITEM 2
Invest in instructors

If you do not take away anything else from this book, I hope that you see the value of this action item. One of the most important factors that contribute to the success of SG Math in Singapore is the teachers, so it is extremely crucial to invest in training for the instructors of SG Math in the U.S.

Singapore's curriculum is designed for trained, professional teachers to use. In Singapore, teaching is a respectable profession. Teachers are selected from the top one-third of their age cohort[76], and as I have discussed previously, they are paid during their training at NIE and are assigned to local schools by MOE after their course. They continue to undergo professional development regularly throughout their career so that they can improve on their instructional methods and be informed of the latest pedagogical tools. Teachers are a top priority in Singapore, as they should be in every education system.

Some American schools explained that one of the main reasons why they decided to drop Singapore's curriculum was that the teachers lack a strong mathematics background to properly teach it.[77] This is concerning to me because it does not seem like the problem lies with the curriculum. No matter which curriculum is implemented, teachers should all have a strong foundation in mathematics, be qualified to teach mathematics, and receive regular professional development. Teachers with a solid mathematics background are going to be able to reorganize their existing curriculum in a logical, coherent fashion, if they have not done so already. When students come to me for help, I never request them to change their current curriculum to Singapore's. That is simply not what they need. Instead, I work with them on their existing instructional materials. I reorganize some topics and integrate Singapore's approaches when I see fit. Children should not have to switch between curricula when teachers are not given sufficient training.

Even if the budget for SG Math at home or at school is small, there are ways to save money on manipulatives and other instructional materials so that you can invest the money on instructor training. The instructor's guide for SG Math is simply not enough to help you teach the curriculum effectively.

Both teachers and parents can enroll in a short seminar course to understand what the curriculum is and how it should be taught. There are even some online courses that you can watch at your own pace. Be sure to vet the training institutes and their experts to make sure that they have a credible background and there is no inaccurate information presented. With a bigger budget, it is even possible to attend seminars and training sessions organized by NIE in Singapore to learn from Singaporean experts. These training sessions and seminars are usually open to anyone, not just teachers, so I highly recommend homeschool parents to attend a short course on SG Math to learn more on how to effectively use it.

ACTION ITEM 3
Drawing bar models is not an option; it's a necessity

Even though the Model Method isn't the only problem-solving strategy taught in SG Math, it is arguably the most important. Bar models are specifically designed to help elementary school children figure out word problems. If children using SG Math do not master the skill of drawing models, they are essentially not using SG Math. In order to teach children how to effectively use bar models to solve word problems, the instructors have to understand how to use them so that they can guide children through the process.

ACTION ITEM 4
Open up the problem-solving process

While it is necessary that children learn how to use bar models to solve problems, it is also critical that they be open to other methods of problem-solving. One strategy that I use with my students is that they first use bar models to solve a problem, and then I challenge them to think of another way to solve the same problem. Sometimes, children can come up with three or more different ways to solve the same question! That is great – let them be creative, but make sure that they include at least one standard way.

ACTION ITEM 5
Focus on processes and teach error analysis

Instructors should always focus on children's mathematical processes, instead of fixating on the final answer, especially at the elementary level. Go through their equations and workings line by line to see if the child has made any conceptual or careless mistakes. When I first start working with a student, I go through their answers with them so that they can observe how I grade their work. This not only helps them get into the habit of checking their own work meticulously in the future, it will also indicate to them that I care about how they got the answer and not just the answer. As you go through the child's work with them, you can also take the opportunity to teach them how to analyze their own errors.

Usually, I would point out to my students where they made a mistake, but I wouldn't tell them what the mistake is. I would then ask them what went wrong and have them identify whether the mistake is a conceptual one or a careless one, and then they correct it. Eventually, I would just tell them which questions they made a mistake in and have them figure out where they made the mistake. This is one of the most essential skills to have that can significantly impact one's mathematical achievements. The ability to check work thoroughly and identify and correct any mistakes made will bump a child's grade up from a B to an A.

ACTION ITEM 6
Engage children in your teaching

Whether you use SG Math or not, math education is not about rote learning. This does not only mean that children need to understand the why's behind their work. It is also about involving children in the teaching and learning process. In Action items 4 and 5, I suggested a few ways to engage a child in the learning process, such as challenging them to come up with different ways to solve one problem or going through their work with an instructor. As I've mentioned in Chapter 3, you can also create a crafting project where you and the child make manipulatives together. I remember one of my teachers gave us the opportunity to make up our own questions for a quiz. Or if you have more than one child in a classroom or at home, have them grade each other's work or take turns to teach the class. There are so many different ways to involve children in the learning and teaching process. What's important is that they get a chance to be in the instructor's shoes or do something hands-on, which will most definitely deepen their conceptual understanding.

ACTION ITEM 7
Encourage children to discuss math

This is related to Action item 6. Encouraging children to discuss math verbally is something that we may not have grown up with ourselves, but it is a crucial component in SG Math's framework. Often times, when we talk through something, we get a clearer picture of the situation, or we are able to figure out what we don't understand. The same thing happens with math – when children talk through math concepts and processes, they are more likely to internalize the content better and identify areas that they are still unsure of. It is also important in my classrooms that math is not a silent subject. Math is not about keeping your head down and scribbling numbers and equations. It should be a school subject where learners can ask questions, challenge proofs, and cast doubts on equations. When children debate about math topics and concepts, they are actively engaging in the process of knowledge production, which is central not only to the field of mathematics but to every academic discipline.

ACTION ITEM 8
Make connections between different topics

Instructors of SG Math must guide children to observe the interconnections between different topics and concepts. Many of the word problems that appear in SG Math require students to make inter-conceptual and intra-conceptual connections and synthesize the various concepts they have learned in different topics. When you teach SG Math, it is imperative that you make explicit comments about how one concept can relate to another and pose questions to students so that they can make their own connections. Concept maps are a useful way to create a visual structure of everything children have learned and to observe unusual connections that may not have been obvious otherwise.

ACTION ITEM 9
Expect children to do well in math

Never tell children that you're not a math person or that they just need to pass math. Children must have a growth mindset and believe that if they work hard and put in the effort, they will be able to improve their math skills. When children hear you imply that math abilities are genetic or that they don't have to do well, they will simply give up when given a more challenging problem. Over time, they will stop trying altogether and accept that they are just not meant to do well in math. Instructors should push children through age-appropriate challenging questions, even if it means to scaffold them with lots of guiding questions. With your help, children will still feel a sense of accomplishment when they solve a difficult problem, so the next time they encounter a challenging problem, they will be more likely to try it and persevere instead of giving up.

ACTION ITEM 10

Let children apply concepts in different contexts

When you are putting together homework or reviews, try to balance routine questions with nonroutine questions and include problems with a varying degree of difficulty. This way, children can apply their knowledge in different contexts, practice basic skills, and also be challenged. Repeating a similar type of question a few times in a worksheet is absolutely fine. Just remember to avoid preparing a mind-numbing worksheet with hundreds of similar questions.

Teaching math to young children is a monumental task, no matter what curriculum you use. It takes a lot of preparation, time, and effort, and sometimes it even requires you to re-learn and think through some of the concepts yourself. But building a solid foundation in math for young children is so important, and it is a task that we, as educators and parents, must undertake. It is our responsibility to show our children that mathematics is not just about numbers and calculations but is, instead, an integrated discipline that has very practical and serious implications on our lives. We have to demonstrate to our children that we are all born with mathematical abilities and that the key to success in math, and in life, is perseverance. Last but not least, if we have learned anything from Singapore's math curriculum, it is that a good math education can only be achieved through education - education of teachers, education of administrators, education of policymakers, and education of parents. It is when all these stakeholders are informed that children can receive quality mathematics instruction, which will open the doors for them to an incredibly bright future.

THE SECRETS TO SINGAPORE'S WORLD-CLASS MATH CURRICULUM

SUMMARIZED

KEY INFORMATION

KEY PLAYERS
- Jerome S. Bruner
- Dr. Kho T. H. & Team
- Jeremy Bloom
- George Pólya
- John Flavell

KEY APPROACHES & FEATURES
- Spiral Curriculum
- Concrete-Pictorial-Abstract Approach
- The Model Method
- School Mathematics Curriculum Framework (SMCF)

MYTHS

1. SG Math is not a spiral curriculum
2. I must buy manipulatives to use SG Math
3. I have to follow exactly the structure of all instructional materials
4. The Model Method is the only way to solve problems in SG Math
5. SG Math looks so simple that children can learn it on their own.

TAKEAWAYS

1. Invest in elementary mathematics education
2. A logically and coherently structured mathematics curriculum is key
3. Emphasize problem-solving processes
4. Procedures are important, but they do not have to be memorized
5. Practice, practice, practice!
6. Integrate test-taking techniques in math lessons
7. Develop children's mathematical mindsets
8. Commit to a curriculum and stay flexible

WHAT CAN WE DO?

1. Do more research
2. Invest in instructors
3. Drawing bar models is not an option; it's a necessity
4. Open up the problem-solving process
5. Focus on processes and teach error analysis
6. Engage children in your teaching
7. Encourage children to discuss math
8. Make connections between different topics
9. Expect children to do well in math
10. Let children apply concepts in different contexts

Notes

1. "Population in Brief 2019 Singapore," Strategy Group, September 2019, https://www.strategygroup.gov.sg/files/media-centre/publications/population-in-brief-2019.pdf.

2. "Environment: Latest Data," Department of Statistics Singapore, last modified August 12, 2020, https://www.singstat.gov.sg/find-data/search-by-theme/society/environment/latest-data.

3. "GDP per capita (current US$) – Singapore," The World Bank Group, accessed November 1, 2020, https://data.worldbank.org/indicator/NY.GDP.PCAP.CD?locations=SG.

4. Ibid.

5. "World Economic Outlook Database," International Monetary Fund, published October 2019, https://www.imf.org/en/Publications/WEO/weo-database/2019/October.

6. Alan Ginsburg et al., *What the United States Can Learn From Singapore's Word-Class Mathematics System (and what Singapore can learn from the United States): An Exploratory Study*, ed. Elizabeth Witt (Washington, DC: American Institutes for Research, 2005).

7. Ginsburg et al., *What the United States Can Learn From Singapore's Word-Class Mathematics System*, 68-96.

8. Singapore Math is the trademark of Singapore Math Inc. and Marshall Cavendish Pte. Ltd.

9. 2. Berinderjeet Kaur, "Overview of Singapore's Education System and Milestones in the Development of the System and School Mathematics Curriculum," in *Mathematics Education in Singapore*, eds. Tin Lam Toh, Berinderjeet Kaur, and Eng Guan Tay, (Singapore: Springer Nature, 2019), 23.

10. Ibid., 25.

11. Ibid., 25.

12. Ibid., 25.

13. Ibid., 28.

14. Ibid., 13-33.

15. Kishore Mahbubani, "Why Singapore is the world's most successful society," Huffington Post, published April 8, 2015, https://www.huffpost.com/entry/singapore-world-successful-society_b_7934988.

16. 3. Ngan Hoe Lee, Wee Leng Ng, and Li Gek Pearlyn Lim, "The Intended School Mathematics Curriculum," in *Mathematics Education in Singapore*, eds. Tin Lam Toh, Berinderjeet Kaur, and Eng Guan Tay, (Singapore: Springer Nature, 2019), 35-54.

17. Jerome S. Bruner, The Process of Education, 6th ed. (Cambridge, Massachusetts: Harvard University Press, 1960), 54.

18. Jerome S. Bruner, *Toward a Theory of Instruction* (Cambridge, Massachusetts: Harvard University Press, 1966), 10-12.

19. Tek Hong Kho, "Mathematical models for solving arithmetic problems," in *Proceedings of Fourth Southeast Asian Conference on Mathematical Education* (Singapore: Institute of Education, 1987), 345-351.

20. 8. Joseph B. W. Yeo et al., "Innovative Pedagogical Practices," in *Mathematics Education in Singapore*, eds. Tin Lam Toh, Berinderjeet Kaur, and Eng Guan Tay (Singapore: Springer Nature, 2019), 169.

21. Tek Hong Kho, Shu Mei Yeo, and James Lim, *The Singapore Model Method for Learning Mathematics*, 10th ed. (Singapore: Marshall Cavendish Education, 2009).

22. Khoon Yoong Wong, "Curriculum Development in Singapore," in *Curriculum Development in East Asia*, eds. Colin Marsh & Paul Morris (London: The Falmer Press, 1991), 129-160.

23. Ministry of Education, *Mathematics syllabus (Lower Secondary)*, (Singapore: author, 1990).

24. Ministry of Education, *Primary mathematics teaching and learning syllabus.* (Singapore: author, 2012a), 16.

25. National Research Council, *Adding It Up: Helping Children Learn Mathematics*, eds. Jeremy Kilpatrick, Jane Swafford, and Bradford Findell (Washington, DC: National Academy Press, 2001).

26. 3. Ngan Hoe Lee, Wee Leng Ng, and Li Gek Pearlyn Lim, "The Intended School Mathematics Curriculum," 37.

27. National Research Council, *Adding It Up,* 120.

28. Richard R. Skemp, "Relational Understanding and Instrumental Understanding," *The Arithmetic Teacher* 26, no. 3 (1978): 9-15, https://www.jstor.org/stable/41187667.

29. George Pólya, *How to Solve It,* 2nd ed. (New York: Doubleday Anchor Books, 1957).

30. 3. Ngan Hoe Lee, Wee Leng Ng, and Li Gek Pearlyn Lim, "The Intended School Mathematics Curriculum," 40.

31. National Research Council, *Adding It Up,* 129.

32. Benjamin S. Bloom, "Learning for Mastery," *Evaluation Comment* (UCLA-CSIEP) 1, no. 2 (1968): 1-12.

33. Mark Keierleber, "6 reasons why Singapore Math might just be the better way," The 74, published July 11, 2015, https://www.the74million.org/article/6-reasons-why-singapore-math-might-just-be-the-better-way/.

34. See examples: Andrew P. Jaciw, Whitney Hegseth, and Megan Toby, "Assessing Impacts of *Math in Focus*, a 'Singapore Math' program," in *Journal of Research on Educational Effectiveness* 9, no. 4 (2016): 473-502, doi: 10.1080/19345747.2016.1164777.; Tina L. Powell, "A comparative analysis of the Singapore Math curriculum and the Everyday Mathematics curriculum on fifth grade achievement in a large northeastern urban public school district," *Seton Hall Univeresity Dissertations and Theses* (2014), https://scholarship.shu.edu/cgi/viewcontent.cgi?article=2999&context=dissertations.

35. See examples: Kevin Mahoney, "Effects of Singapore's Model Method on elementary student problem solving performance: single subject research," *Northeastern University Education Doctoral Theses* (2012), http://hdl.handle.net/2047/d20002962.; Jenny Taliaferro Blalock, "The impact of Singapore Math on student knowledge and enjoyment in mathematics," *Louisiana Tech Doctoral Dissertations* (2011), https://digitalcommons.latech.edu/cgi/viewcontent.cgi?article=1375&context=dissertations.

36. Kuan Yew Lee, *Speech by Mr. Lee Kuan Yew, Senior Minister, for Africa Leadership forum at the Regent Hotel on Monday, 8 November 1993*, http://www.nas.gov.sg/archivesonline/data/pdfdoc/lky19931108.pdf.

37. Pak Tee Ng, *Learning from Singapore: The power of paradoxes*, 1st ed. (New York: Routledge, 2017), 50-51.

38. Ibid., 50.

39. Fareed Zakaria, "We All Have a Lot to Learn," *Newsweek*, published January 8, 2006, https://www.newsweek.com/we-all-have-lot-learn-108305.

40. U.S. Congress, Public Law 96-88, 1979

41. Ginsburg et al., *What the United States Can Learn From Singapore's Word-Class Mathematics System.*

42. See examples: "What is Singapore Math." Singapore Math Inc., https://www.singaporemath.com/what-is-singapore-math/.; "What is maths mastery?," Maths No Problem!, https://mathsnoproblem.com/en/mastery/what-is-maths-mastery/.

43. The University of Chicago School Mathematics Project, *Everyday mathematics for parents: what you need to know to help your child succeed* (Chicago: The University of Chicago Press, 2017), 10-11

44. Hairon Salleh, "A Qualitative Study of Singapore Primary School Teachers' Conceptions of Educational Change," *Teaching and Learning* 24, no. 2 (2003): 105-115, https://repository.nie.edu.sg/bitstream/10497/315/1/TL-24-2-105.pdf.

45. Bloom, "Learning for Mastery," 1-12.

46. Barry Garelick, "Miracle Math: A successful program from Singapore tests the limits of school reform in the subrubs," *Education Next* 6, no. 4 (2006): 38-45, https://www.educationnext.org/miracle-math/.

47. Kathy Hirsh-Pasek, Roberta Michnick Golinkoff, and Diane Eyer, *Einstein never used flash cards: How our children really learn – and why they need to play more and memorize less* (Pennsylvania: Rodale Books, 2003), 145.

48. Lev Vygotsky, Mind in Society: The Development of Higher Psychological Processes (Cambridge: Harvard University Press, 1978), 87.

49   "Scaffolding and the Zone of Proximal Development," Barefoot TEFL Teacher (blog). Accessed November 1, 2020, https://barefoottefIteacher.com/blog/scaffolding-zone-of-proximal-development.

50   Mark Keierleber, "6 reasons why Singapore Math might just be the better way."

51   "Singapore," UNESCO Institute for Statistics, accessed November 1, 2020, http://uis.unesco.org/en/country/sg.

52   "Singapore Economy," Department of Statistics Singapore, last updated July 2020, https://www.singstat.gov.sg/modules/infographics/economy. *SGD dollar amount converted to USD.

53   Garelick, "Miracle Math."

54   Hung-Hsi Wu, "What's Sophisticated about Elementary Mathematics?: Plenty – That's why elementary schools need math teachers," *American Educator* 33, no. 3 (2009): 4-14, https://math.berkeley.edu/~wu/wu2009.pdf.

55   Ibid.

56   Kathy Hirsh-Pasek, Roberta Michnick Golinkoff, and Diane Eyer, *Einstein never used flash cards,* 42-43.

57   Nikki Graf, Richard Fry, and Cary Funk, "7 facts about the STEM workforce," Pew Research Center, published January 9, 2018, https://www.pewresearch.org/fact-tank/2018/01/09/7-facts-about-the-stem-workforce/.

58   Ibid.

59   Ibid.

60   ESA calculations using Current Population Survey public-use microdata and estimates from the Employment Projections Program of the Bureau of Labor Statistics.

61   Madge Goldman, preface to *Singapore Primary Mathematics 1A Teacher's Guide* (Rosenbaum Foundation, 2001).

62   Bill Gates, "Training your brain for recall," GatesNotes, published September 12, 2012, https://www.gatesnotes.com/books/moonwalking-with-einstein.

63   International Organization for Standardization, *ISO 9001:2015 Quality Management Systems - Requirements,* (Geneva, Switzerland: ISO, 2015).

64   Pólya, *How to Solve It.*

65   Ginsburg et al., What the United States Can Learn From Singapore's Word-Class Mathematics System.

66   National Research Council, *Adding It Up,* 121.

67   Ng, *Learning from Singapore,* 107.

68   Bob Hogan and Char Forsten, *8-Step Model Drawing: Singapore's Best Problem-Solving Math Strategies*, 1st ed. (Crystal Springs Books, 2007).

69   Alexander Borisovich, "How the incompetent enlightens the ignorant," accessed November 1, 2020, https://math.berkeley.edu/~giventh/diagnosis.pdf

70   Ng, *Learning from Singapore,* 108.

NOTES

71. Berinderjeet Kaur, "The model method: A tool for representing and visualizing relationships," in *Conference proceedings of ICMI Study 23: Primary mathematics study on whole numbers,* eds. X. Sun, B. Kaur, and J Novotna (2015): 448-455, http://www.umac.mo/fed/ICMI23/doc/Proceedings_ICMI_STUDY_23_final.pdf.

72. See examples: Carol S Dweck, *Mindsets and Math/Science Achievement* (2008), http://www.growthmindsetmaths.com/uploads/2/3/7/7/23776169/mindset_and_math_science_achievement_-_nov_2013.pdf.; Anke Heyder et al., "Teachers' belief that math requires innate ability predicts lower intrinsic motivation among low-achieving students," in *Learning and Instruction* 65, (2020): 1-10, https://doi.org/10.1016/j.learninstruc.2019.101220

73. Jo Boaler, "The Power of Mistakes and Struggle," in *Mathematical Mindsets: Unleashing students' potential through creative math, inspiring messages and innovative teaching* (California: Jossey-Bass, 2016), 11-20.

74. 6. Berinderjeet Kaur, Ying Zhu, and Wai Kwong Cheang, "Singapore's participation in International Benchmark Studies – TIMSS, PISA," in *Mathematics Education in Singapore,* eds. Tin Lam Toh, Berinderjeet Kaur, and Eng Guan Tay (Singapore: Springer Nature, 2019), 119-124.

75. Ibid.

76. Michael Barber, Chinezi Chijoke, and Mona Mourshed, "How the World's Most Improved School Systems Keep Getting Better," McKinsey & Company, published November 1, 2010, https://www.mckinsey.com/industries/public-and-social-sector/our-insights/how-the-worlds-most-improved-school-systems-keep-getting-better#.

77. See examples: Winnie Hu, "Making Math Lessons as Easy as 1, Pause, 2, Pause …," The New York Times, published September 30, 2010, https://www.nytimes.com/2010/10/01/education/01math.html.; Garelick, "Miracle Math."

Bibliography

Barber, Michael, Chinezi Chijoke, and Mona Mourshed. "How the World's Most Improved School Systems Keep Getting Better." McKinsey & Company, published November 1, 2010. https://www.mckinsey.com/industries/public-and-social-sector/our-insights/how-the-worlds-most-improved-school-systems-keep-getting-better#.

Bloom, Benjamin S. "Learning for Mastery." *Evaluation Comment* (UCLA-CSIEP) I, no. 2 (1968): 1-12.

Boaler, Jo. "The Power of Mistakes and Struggle." In *Mathematical Mindsets: Unleashing students' potential through creative math, inspiring messages and innovative teaching*, 11-20. California: Jossey-Bass, 2016.

Borisovich, Alexander. *"How the incompetent enlightens the ignorant,"* accessed November 1, 2020, https://math.berkeley.edu/~giventh/diagnosis.pdf.

Bruner, Jerome S. *The Process of Education*, 6th edition. Cambridge, Massachusetts: Harvard University Press, 1960.

Bruner, Jerome S. *Toward a Theory of Instruction*. Cambridge, Massachusetts: Harvard University Press, 1966.

"Environment: Latest Data." Department of Statistics Singapore, last modified August 12, 2020. https://www.singstat.gov.sg/find-data/search-by-theme/society/environment/latest-data.

Garelick, Barry. "Miracle Math: A successful program from Singapore tests the limits of school reform in the suburbs." *Education Next* 6, no. 4 (2006): 38-45 https://www.educationnext.org/miracle-math/.

Gates, Bill. "Training your brain for recall." GatesNotes, published September 12, 2012. https://www.gatesnotes.com/books/moonwalking-with-einstein.

"GDP per capita (current US$ - Singapore." The World Bank Group, accessed November 1, 2020. https://data.worldbank.org/indicator/NY.GDP.PCAP.CD?locations=SG.

Ginsburg, Alan, Steven Leinwand, Terry Anstrom, and Elizabeth Pollock. *What the United States Can Learn From Singapore's Word-Class Mathematics System (and what Singapore can learn from the United States): An Exploratory Study*, edited by Elizabeth Witt. Washington, DC: American Institutes for Research, 2005.

Goldman, Madge. Preface to *Singapore Primary Mathematics 1A Teacher's Guide*. Rosenbaum Foundation, 2001.

Graf, Nikki, Richard Fry, and Cary Funk. "7 facts about the STEM workforce." Pew Research Center, published January 9, 2018. https://www.pewresearch.org/fact-tank/2018/01/09/7-facts-about-the-stem-workforce/.

Hirsh-Pasek, Kathy, Roberta Michnick Golinkoff, and Diane Eyer. *Einstein never used flash cards: How our children really learn – and why they need to play more and memorize less*. Pennsylvania: Rodale Books, 2003.

International Organization for Standardization. *ISO 9001:2015 Quality Management Systems – Requirements*. Geneva, Switzerland: ISO, 2015.

Hogan, Bob and Char Forsten. *8-Step Model Drawing: Singapore's Best Problem-Solving Math Strategies*, 1st ed. Crystal Springs Books, 2007.

Kaur, Berinderjeet. "The model method: A tool for representing and visualizing relationships." In *Conference proceedings of ICMI Study 23: Primary mathematics study on whole numbers*, edited by X. Sun, B. Kaur, and J Novotna, (2015): 448-455. http://www.umac.mo/fed/ICMI23/doc/Proceedings_ICMI_STUDY_23_final.pdf

Kaur, Berinderjeet. "Overview of Singapore's Education System and Milestones in the Development of the System and School Mathematics Curriculum." In *Mathematics Education in Singapore,* edited by Tin Lam Toh, Berinderjeet Kaur, and Eng Guan Tay, 13-34. Singapore: Springer Nature, 2019.

Kaur, Berinderjeet, Ying Zhu, and Wai Kwong Cheang. "Singapore's participation in International Benchmark Studies – TIMSS, PISA." In *Mathematics Education in Singapore,* edited by Tin Lam Toh, Berinderjeet Kaur, and Eng Guan Tay, 119-124. Singapore: Springer Nature, 2019.

Keierleber, Mark. "6 reasons why Singapore Math might just be the better way." The 74, published July 11, 2015. https://www.the74million.org/article/6-reasons-why-singapore-math-might-just-be-the-better-way/.

Kho, Tek Hong. "Mathematical models for solving arithmetic problems." In *Proceedings of Fourth Southeast Asian Conference on Mathematical Education,* 345-351. Singapore: Institute of Education, 1987.

Kho, Tek Hong, Shu Mei Yeo, and James Lim. *The Singapore Model Method for Learning Mathematics,* 10th ed. Singapore: Marshall Cavendish Education, 2009.

BIBLIOGRAPHY

Lee, Kuan Yew. *Speech by Mr. Lee Kuan Yew, Senior Minister, for Africa Leadership forum at the Regent Hotel on Monday, 8 November 1993*. http://www.nas.gov.sg/archivesonline/data/pdfdoc/lky19931108.pdf.

Lee, Ngan Hoe, Wee Leng Ng, and Li Gek Pearlyn Lim, "The Intended School Mathematics Curriculum." In *Mathematics Education in Singapore*, edited by Tin Lam Toh, Berinderjeet Kaur, and Eng Guan Tay, 35-54. Singapore: Springer Nature, 2019.

Mahbubani, Kishore. "Why Singapore is the world's most successful society." Huffington Post, published April 8, 2015. https://www.huffpost.com/entry/singapore-world-successful-society_b_7934988.

Ministry of Education. *Mathematics syllabus* (Lower Secondary). Singapore: author, 1990.

Ministry of Education. *Primary mathematics teaching and learning syllabus*. Singapore: author, 2012a.

National Research Council. *Adding It Up: Helping Children Learn Mathematics*, edited by Jeremy Kilpatrick, Jane Swafford, and Bradford Findell. Washington, DC: National Academy Press, 2001.

Ng, Pak Tee. *Learning from Singapore: The power of paradoxes*, 1st ed. New York: Routledge, 2017.

Pólya, George. *How to Solve It*, 2nd ed. New York: Doubleday Anchor Books, 1957.

"Population in Brief 2019 Singapore." Strategy Group, September 2019. https://www.strategygroup.gov.sg/files/media-centre/publications/population-in-brief-2019.pdf.

Salleh, Hairon. "A Qualitative Study of Singapore Primary School Teachers' Conceptions of Educational Change." *Teaching and Learning* 24, no. 2 (2003): 105-115, https://repository.nie.edu.sg/bitstream/10497/315/1/TL-24-2-105.pdf.

"Scaffolding and the Zone of Proximal Development." Barefoot TEFL Teacher. Accessed November 1, 2020. https://barefootteflteacher.com/blog/scaffolding-zone-of-proximal-development.

"Singapore." UNESCO Institute for Statistics. Accessed November 1, 2020. http://uis.unesco.org/en/country/sg.

"Singapore Economy." Department of Statistics Singapore, last updated July 2020. https://www.singstat.gov.sg/modules/infographics/economy.

Skemp, Richard R. "Relational Understanding and Instrumental Understanding." *The Arithmetic Teacher* 26, no. 3 (1978): 9-15. https://www.jstor.org/stable/41187667.

The University of Chicago School Mathematics Project. *Everyday mathematics for parents: what you need to know to help your child succeed*. Chicago: The University of Chicago Press, 2017.

U.S. Congress. Public Law 96-88. 1979.

Vygotsky, Lev. *Mind in Society: The Development of Higher Psychological Processes.* Cambridge: Harvard University Press, 1978.

Wong, Khoon Yoong. "Curriculum Development in Singapore." In *Curriculum Development in East Asia,* edited by Colin Marsh & Paul Morris, 129-160. London: The Falmer Press, 1991.

"World Economic Outlook Database." International Monetary Fund, published October 2019. https://www.imf.org/en/Publications/WEO/weo-database/2019/October.

Wu, Hung-Hsi. "What's Sophisticated about Elementary Mathematics?: Plenty – That's why elementary schools need math teachers." *American Educator* 33, no. 3 (2009): 4-14. https://math.berkeley.edu/~wu/wu2009.pdf.

Yeo, Joseph B. W., Ban Heng Choy, Li Gek Pearlyn Lim and Lai Fong Wong. "Innovative Pedagogical Practices." In *Mathematics Education in Singapore,* eds. Tin Lam Toh, Berinderjeet Kaur, and Eng Guan Tay, 165-194. Singapore: Springer Nature, 2019.

Zakaria, Fareed. "We All Have a Lot to Learn." Newsweek, published January 8, 2006. https://www.newsweek.com/we-all-have-lot-learn-108305.